MODERN STENCILS

35 COLORFUL PROJECTS FOR FURNITURE, TEXTILES, FLOORS, WALLS, AND MORE

NICOLETTE TABRAM

CICO BOOKS
LONDON NEW YORK

Published in 2018 by CICO Books
An imprint of Ryland Peters & Small Ltd
20–21 Jockey's Fields   341 E 116th St
London WC1R 4BW   New York, NY 10029

www.rylandpeters.com

10 9 8 7 6 5 4 3 2 1

A CIP catalog record for this book is available from the Library
of Congress and the British Library.

ISBN: 978 1 78249 549 9

Printed in China

Editor: Amy Christian
Designer: Elizabeth Healey
Photographer: Terry Benson
Stencil designs: Nicolette Tabram
Stylist: Jess Contomichalos

In-house editor: Anna Galkina
Art director: Sally Powell
Head of production: Patricia Harrington
Publishing manager: Penny Craig
Publisher: Cindy Richards

CONTENTS

introduction

A few years ago, after leaving my job as a designer in the fashion industry, I began painting furniture as a way to disconnect from my computer and re-engage with paint and brushes. My whole career has involved working with pattern. I soon began to miss the interest that it can add to a project and so I hand-cut a stencil to use on the doors of a cupboard I was working on.

Before long, I had designed a whole range of stencils and had begun to use them on any surface available to me, including furniture, fabric, floors, stairs, and wallpaper. My love of stencils comes not only from my love of pattern, but is also due to their versatility and ease of use. The most basic of items can be transformed into something of real individuality with the addition of some simple stenciled pattern.

When I'm working on a project in my studio, I become completely absorbed in the process. In the workshops I run, people often comment on the therapeutic effects of a few hours spent stenciling. In these hectic, achievement-driven times I believe that a little stenciling is good for the soul!

The style of stenciling used in this book is clean and modern. Inspiration comes from many sources, though my travels and the things I have collected along the way often provide a rich source of ideas.

Some of the 35 projects are quick and simple while others will require a little more time, but, by following a few basic rules, they are all achievable, whether you are a stencil novice or an old hand.

In addition to the step-by-step guides, you will also find lots of tips and techniques. If you are a beginner, you may find it helpful to practice on paper beforehand.

For some of the projects I have used a tape measure, but you don't need to be too rigid about measuring everything—I often judge the placement of the stencil by eye. The most important thing is to relax and enjoy the process. I genuinely believe that part of the charm of a pattern created with a stencil is that there will be small imperfections—that is a good thing! This is a technique created by hand and, after all, you are a human being and not a machine.

Although each of the stencils on pages 116–125 is used for a specific project, and is labeled accordingly, they can be used in many ways. Once your confidence builds, you can develop your own projects using pattern combinations and color palettes of your choice. I hope that, like me, you too will fall in love with stencils once you have completed a few of the projects in this book.

HAPPY STENCILING!

Nicolette

tools
AND MATERIALS

You only need a few essential tools for a stencil kit, and some of those are standard household items, but I would recommend investing in a few basics: a good craft knife with a supply of blades, a cutting mat, and a can of spray adhesive. The adhesive may seem expensive, but it will last for a very long time.

MYLAR® OR CARDSTOCK

My preferred medium for stencils is Mylar®. It is transparent, so it makes repositioning stencils for all-over patterns much easier, and, with care, it can be washed and used repeatedly (see page 11). It is available in a range of thicknesses, which are measured in microns. The higher the number of microns, the thicker the material will be. Lightweight Mylar® is easier to cut, but if it is too thin, the stencil will be flimsy, making it harder to work with. It will not last as long as a stencil cut from a heavier Mylar®. For hand-cut stencils, I would recommend using a weight of around 125 microns.

If you are using cardstock, I would recommend choosing a weight of around 32lb (200–250gsm) as, again, lighter weights will not last as long, and heavier weights will be difficult to cut. Cardstock is a good medium for single motifs, but more difficult to use when working with repeating patterns, as it is opaque and can't be washed. For more information on how to cut a stencil, see page 10.

PAINT

A variety of paints can be used with stencils, but the key considerations are the opacity and the consistency. Paints that are too thin will bleed underneath the stencil and paints which are too thick will be difficult to apply and cause "pooling" around the edges of the holes in the stencil.

PAINT FOR STENCILING FURNITURE

Specialist stencil and acrylic paints, including those with metallic finishes, work well on furniture, as they are waterproof, dry quickly, and create a smooth, crisp edge. Most of these paints are available in small pots, which is useful, as stenciling usually requires very little paint.

Furniture paints can also be used but it is important that they are the correct consistency: too thick, and they will be hard to apply; too thin, and they will bleed.

PAINT FOR STENCILING FABRIC

Acrylic paint and some stencil paint can work very successfully on fabric, but bear in mind that these paints will sit on top of, rather than sink into, the fibers of the fabric. This slightly rougher finish is fine for heavier fabrics, such as drapes (curtains), upholstery, and canvas bags. For items such as bed linen or scarves, where a smoother finish is required, I prefer to use fabric screen-printing inks. These contain a binder, which creates a gel-like consistency, making them very easy to work with. After the fabric has been pressed with a hot iron, it can be machine-washed to remove the binder, creating a lovely soft handle. Some fabric paints can also be used, provided they are not too runny.

PAINT FOR STENCILING FLOORS

Any paint which is suitable for stenciling onto hard surfaces can be used on floors, provided a couple of coats of hard-wearing varnish are applied over the top. I usually use my stencil paint for floors as it is suitable for internal and external use, and so is very hardwearing.

VARNISH

When stenciling over furniture paint, I always apply a coat of varnish before adding the stencil pattern. This protects the porous surface as you work on it and allows for any mistakes to be quickly wiped away. Once the pattern has been added an additional coat of varnish can be painted onto the whole piece.

Water-based varnish is much easier to work with and dries quickly. I prefer a matte finish, though satin or high gloss finishes are also available.

STENCIL PASTE

This is a thick, white substance which can be used with stencils to create a 3D relief effect. Once dry, it forms a very hard, decorative surface which can be painted over.

STENCIL BRUSHES

Stencil brushes are round with a flat top, with strong, flexible bristles, and are available in a selection of sizes. Smaller brushes are useful when working on narrow borders or multi-colored projects where small elements need to be picked out. For most of my projects, I use a size 8 brush as this larger size allows the paint to be applied more quickly.

It is worth investing in the correct brushes for your projects. They are not expensive and, as they are specifically designed for the job, you will achieve more successful results.

SPRAY ADHESIVE

I always apply a spray adhesive to the back of my stencils as it significantly reduces the chance of the paint bleeding underneath and spoiling the results.

Shake the can well before use, hold the stencil at arm's length, then apply a light, even coat to the back of the stencil, allowing a few seconds for it to dry. The stencil can be repositioned on the surface several times before it is necessary to reapply the adhesive.

Ideally, spray adhesive should be used outside, but, if you do not have easy access to an outside space, holding the stencil inside a large plastic bag while spraying will help to contain the adhesive.

LOW TACK TAPE

This can be used as an alternative to spray adhesive, and is preferable to using a standard masking tape, which may leave behind a sticky residue on the surface. To use, simply stick a small strip on either side of the stencil.

OTHER USEFUL EQUIPMENT

- Plastic pots with lids for storing mixed paint colors
- Tape measure
- Pencil
- Sticky notes
- Paper towels
- Baby wipes—these are great for wiping away mistakes and keeping hands clean

For more information, see Resources on page 126.

basic
TECHNIQUES

It is important to change the scalpel blade as soon as it becomes blunt. A sharp blade is much easier to work with and will produce smoother lines.

If you are cutting your stencil from cardstock, the procedure is the same, but you will need to spray the back of the template and lay it on top of the cardstock. Once the stencil is cut, remove the template and discard.

Cutting Mylar® requires a reasonable amount of pressure. You may wish to practice on a scrap piece before cutting the actual stencil.

CUTTING A STENCIL

Templates for all the stencils used in the book can be found on pages 116–125. I recommend that you cut stencils from Mylar® (see page 8). They can also be cut from cardstock or even paper, though these are not suitable materials if you wish to use the stencil repeatedly or for multi-colored projects, as they cannot be washed.

EQUIPMENT

STENCIL TEMPLATE

SHEETS OF MYLAR®

PHOTOCOPIER OR SCANNER
AND PRINTER

COPY PAPER

SPRAY ADHESIVE

CUTTING MAT

SCALPEL OR CRAFT KNIFE

MAGIC OR CLEAR TAPE
(OPTIONAL)

1 | Select the template for the stencil you would like to cut. Make sure that your sheet of Mylar® is large enough for the template to fit, remembering that the templates are all printed at 50%.

2 | Photocopy (or scan and print) the template onto copy paper rather than cutting the original. To recreate the projects in this book, you will need to enlarge the template by 200%, but the scale of the templates can be enlarged or reduced as desired.

3 | Lightly coat one side of the Mylar® with spray adhesive, then place it on top of the paper template and smooth carefully.

4 | Working on the cutting mat, position the blade of your scalpel or craft knife on the first line you are going to cut. Pierce the surface of the Mylar® with the point of the blade before cutting along the lines. This will help to prevent the scalpel or knife from slipping.

5 | Work your way carefully around the design, holding the Mylar® steady with your free hand. Turn the template as necessary, rather than trying to twist your arm into uncomfortable positions. Remove each piece of Mylar® as you cut out the shapes. You will probably cut through the template in places, which is why I advise using a photocopy.

6 | Once you have cut out the whole stencil, trim off any rough edges with the scalpel and repair any mistakes with small pieces of tape if required. If necessary, trim the edges of the tape with the scalpel. Remove the paper template and discard.

PREPARING THE SURFACE

Very little preparation of surfaces is necessary for stencil projects; the most important thing is that they are clean and dust-free.

Furniture should be wiped down with a cloth and warm, soapy water to remove any dust or stains, particularly if you are using old pieces.

Floors should be thoroughly vacuumed to remove any loose debris, then washed with warm water and a suitable floor cleaner.

Fabrics need to be clean and without creases.

LOADING THE STENCIL BRUSH

It is important to use a dry brush, so that the paint does not become diluted and bleed underneath the stencil.

Overloading the brush with paint is the most common mistake when working with stencils. This is a problem, as an excess of paint is likely to seep underneath the stencil.

Dip the tip of the bristles into the pot of paint and remove as much paint as possible on the side of the pot, on a piece of paper, or on the corner of the stencil, pushing the brush down and rotating the bristles to ensure that the paint is evenly distributed. When working on fabric, you will not need to remove quite as much paint (or ink), as the surface is quite absorbent.

APPLYING THE PAINT

Hold the stencil in position with one hand. Place the brush on the stencil at a slight angle, push down, and rotate in a small circular movement, applying the paint through the holes. As the paint is applied so thinly, it will dry almost immediately and the stencil can be lifted and repositioned straight away. If there is an excess of paint, carefully lay a clean piece of paper over the image and gently tap down to blot the paint.

TIP

Stenciling can produce intricate results and yet the actual process is very simple. Build your confidence by practicing on paper if you are a beginner.

WASHING MYLAR® STENCILS

Mylar® is a robust material which can be washed repeatedly. Soak the stencil for a short time in warm, soapy water before gently scrubbing with a brush or soft cloth. Some paints will leave a residue even after washing, particularly acrylic paint. This is not a problem, as the paint is waterproof.

Fabric screen-printing ink or fabric paint should be washed off completely. These are not waterproof and therefore, if not properly removed, the color will bleed the next time the stencil is used. Don't worry if the color has stained the stencil, it is just the excess that needs to be removed.

CHAPTER 1

FURNITURE
AND ACCESSORIES

GRAPHIC *floral chair*

Painted and stenciled chairs are a lovely way to add a little color to a room. A group of mismatched wooden chairs can be unified with paint and stencils to create a set for a dining table. I have a bright green stenciled chair in my white studio—even a single chair at a desk can add real personality to a room. This project uses a simple graphic floral stencil with a cool Mediterranean color palette of blue and white. If you want a more natural option, add the stencil pattern directly to the wood and finish with a couple of coats of varnish.

MATERIALS AND EQUIPMENT

STENCIL (TEMPLATE ON PAGE 118)

WOODEN CHAIR

CLOTH

BRUSHES FOR PAINT AND VARNISH

BLUE FURNITURE PAINT

MATTE FINISH WATER-BASED VARNISH

TAPE MEASURE AND PENCIL
(OPTIONAL)

SPRAY ADHESIVE OR LOW TACK TAPE

STENCIL BRUSH

WHITE STENCIL PAINT

TIP

The position of the stencil does not always need to be completely accurate. It adds a certain charm if the placement of the pattern is a little imperfect.

1 | Using the template on page 118, prepare the stencil following the instructions on page 10.

2 | Wipe the chair with a damp cloth to remove any dirt or greasy marks, then apply two coats of furniture paint. Allow to dry, before applying a coat of water-based varnish. Let dry.

3 Position the stencil by eye, or use a tape measure to find the center point. Mark it very lightly with a pencil and use this as a guide for the position of the first motif. Lightly coat the back of the stencil with spray adhesive. Position the stencil on the surface of the chair and smooth down. Alternatively, tape it in position.

4 Dip the tip of the stencil brush into the white stencil paint and remove as much paint as possible on the side of the pot. Apply the paint in a small circular motion through the holes in the stencil.

5 Lift the stencil and repeat for the other three sections. As the paint dries very quickly, there is no need to wait before repositioning the stencil.

6 Paint another coat of varnish onto the seat of the chair and let dry. Once the varnish is dry, the chair is ready to use.

5

6

DECORATIVE
nightstand

This varnished pine cabinet has been transformed with a couple of coats of paint and a tile-inspired stencil. Even with my love of decoration, I wouldn't necessarily advocate a room filled with patterned furniture, but one statement piece can create a real centerpiece. In this case, a pair of stenciled nightstands would look stunning. The stencil for this project works well on any size of cabinet; simply start at the center point of each panel and work outward, allowing the pattern to overlap the edges.

MATERIALS AND EQUIPMENT

STENCILS 1 AND 2 (TEMPLATES ON PAGE 119)

CABINET

CLOTH

BRUSHES FOR PAINT AND VARNISH

BLUE FURNITURE PAINT

MATTE FINISH WATER-BASED VARNISH

TAPE MEASURE AND PENCIL

SPRAY ADHESIVE OR LOW TACK TAPE

STENCIL BRUSH

WHITE STENCIL PAINT

1 | Using the templates on page 119, prepare the stencils following the instructions on page 10.

2 | Wipe down all surfaces with a damp cloth to remove any dirt or greasy marks, and unscrew any handles. Apply two coats of furniture paint and let dry.

3 | When the paint has dried, apply a coat of varnish to all painted surfaces and let dry.

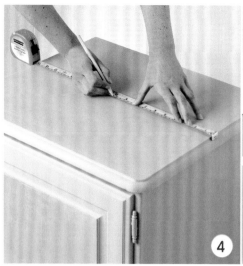

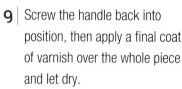

4 | Using a tape measure, find the center point on the top of the cabinet and lightly mark with a pencil. Measure both the width and depth for accuracy.

5 | Lightly coat the back of Stencil 1 with spray adhesive. Position the stencil in the center of the surface and smooth down. Alternatively, tape it in position.

6 | Dip the tip of the stencil brush into the stencil paint. Remove as much paint as possible on the side of the pot before applying in a circular motion through the holes.

7 | Carefully lift the stencil, reposition, and continue until the whole surface is covered with pattern. Repeat the same process on the sides and door of the cabinet, starting from the center point each time.

8 | Add the border around the outer edge of the door using the diamond stencil (Stencil 2). Turn the stencil 90 degrees to continue the pattern around the corners, overlapping the last painted diamond shape. You may need to play around with the positioning of the diamonds to fit your door. I increased the space between the shapes as I neared the end, in order to achieve a complete diamond on each corner.

9 | Screw the handle back into position, then apply a final coat of varnish over the whole piece and let dry.

TIPS

For this project I used furniture paint, which can be applied directly onto varnished surfaces. Always remember to check the instructions on the can.

By sealing the paint with varnish before adding the pattern, it is possible to quickly wipe away any stenciled mishaps with a damp cloth.

FURNITURE AND ACCESSORIES

concrete
PLANTER

The simple lines of this concrete planter work beautifully with an ornate, Indian-inspired motif stencil. There is something particularly satisfying about stenciling onto concrete because the smooth surface is perfect for achieving a crisp and clean stenciled image. I have something similar on the windowsill by my front door—people visiting for the first time know that they are at the right house!

MATERIALS AND EQUIPMENT

STENCIL (TEMPLATE ON PAGE 117)

CONCRETE PLANTER—THE ONE USED HERE IS 20IN (50CM) WIDE

SPRAY ADHESIVE OR LOW TACK TAPE

TAPE MEASURE

STENCIL BRUSH

WHITE STENCIL PAINT

1 | Using the template on page 117, prepare the stencil following the instructions on page 10.

2 | Lightly coat the back of the stencil with spray adhesive. Place the stencil roughly in the center of the planter. Alternatively, tape it in position. Hold the tape measure across the width of the planter and, if necessary, adjust the position of the stencil so that it is centered.

3 | Dip the tip of the stencil brush into the paint and remove as much as possible on the side of the pot. Using small circular movements, apply the paint through the holes in the stencil.

4 | Lift the stencil and reposition on the left side so that the tips of the outer flower are almost touching the same flower on the first motif. Apply the paint as before, then repeat on the other side.

TIP

It is particularly important to have very little paint on the brush when stenciling onto hard surfaces.

INLAY EFFECT
cabinet

I found this cabinet in a local thrift store, covered in cobwebs and painted with white gloss. It was badly chipped (not in a good way!) and in need of a makeover. I have used three different border stencils, inspired by the wonderful bone inlay furniture which I have admired so much on my trips to India. The layout of the design has been specifically devised to fit the dimensions of this cabinet, but can be adapted to fit any size. Don't worry about achieving perfection—there will be areas that don't match up properly or are not perfectly symmetrical, but that is all part of the charm of a handcrafted product. You can use little elements from the stencils to fill in any gaps in your layout. This pattern also look beautiful when applied directly to bare wood.

MATERIALS AND EQUIPMENT

STENCILS 1, 2, AND 3 (TEMPLATES ON
PAGE 120 AND 119)

WOODEN CABINET

CLOTH

BRUSHES FOR PAINT AND VARNISH

BLUE FURNITURE PAINT

MATTE FINISH WATER-BASED VARNISH

SPRAY ADHESIVE OR LOW TACK TAPE

STICKY NOTES

STENCIL BRUSH

WHITE STENCIL PAINT

1 | Using the templates on pages 120 and 119, prepare the stencils following the instructions on page 10.

2 | Wipe down the surfaces of the cabinet with a damp cloth to remove any dirt or greasy marks. Pull out the drawers and stand them on the floor. If possible, remove any drawer handles. (This makes it easier to paint and stencil the surface, but is not essential.)

3 | Apply two coats of furniture paint to the cabinet, drawer fronts, and the interior of the cabinet doors. Let dry.

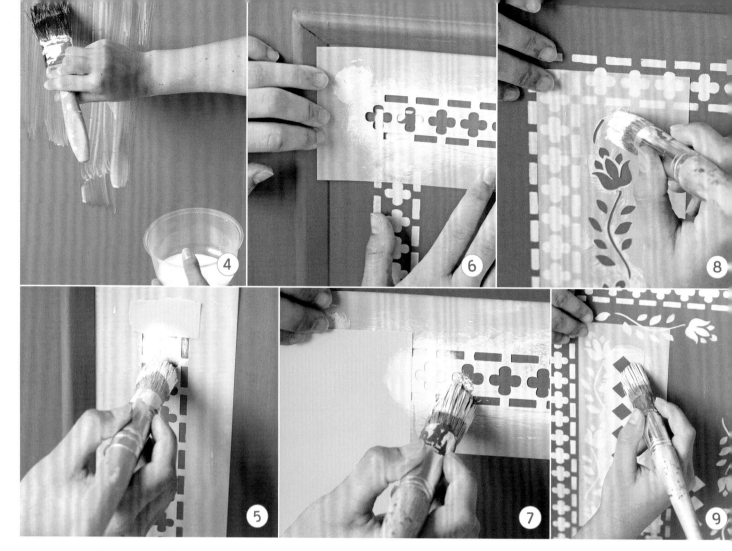

4 When the paint has dried, apply a coat of varnish to all painted surfaces and let dry.

5 Lightly coat the back of Stencil 1 with spray adhesive. Position the stencil in the corner of the first door panel using the edge of the stencil as a guide. Alternatively, tape it in position. Place a small piece of sticky note over the top of the border so that it cuts off the top of the central shape. Dip the tip of the stencil brush into the stencil paint and remove as much paint as possible on the side of the pot. Using a small circular motion, apply the paint through the holes in the stencil.

6 Rotate the stencil 90 degrees and position it at the top of the painted design to create the corner of the border, as shown above.

7 Mask the areas already painted with a sticky note. Apply the paint as before, then continue until the outer border is complete. You may have to increase or decrease the spacing slightly between the shapes as you near completion so that the design fits.

8 Using Stencil 2 in the same way, continue to fill the panel, referring to the photographs for guidance on positioning.

9 Before using Stencil 1 again to fill the center of the panel, add a diamond border using Stencil 3. Repeat the design on the second door panel.

10 Apply Stencil 1 (the outer border) across the width of each drawer at the top and bottom. Rotate the stencil 90 degrees, then add the pattern at the sides, using a sticky note to mask the borders at the top and bottom. Fill in the central areas of each of the drawers with sections of Stencil 2.

11 | Finally, apply a further coat of varnish and let the cabinet dry before replacing the drawers.

TIP

Apply two coats of varnish to the top surface of the cabinet to give it extra protection.

STEP
stool

I love these step stools and probably have far too many for one household, but they are such useful and versatile little items. The plain surface just screams stencils to me, but then I am a bit obsessed! The use of bright green paint and the Moroccan-inspired stencil adds real character to this plain stool and, of course, you can paint it any color you choose.

MATERIALS AND EQUIPMENT

STENCIL (TEMPLATE ON PAGE 122)

WOODEN STEP STOOL—THE ONE USED HERE IS 14IN (35CM WIDE)

CLOTH (OPTIONAL)

BRUSHES FOR PAINT AND VARNISH

GREEN FURNITURE PAINT

MATTE FINISH WATER-BASED VARNISH

SPRAY ADHESIVE OR LOW TACK TAPE

STENCIL BRUSH

STENCIL PAINT IN A NEUTRAL COLOR

1 | Using the template on page 122, prepare the stencil following the instructions on page 10.

2 | Assemble the stool if necessary, following the manufacturer's instructions. If you are using an old stool, wipe it down with a damp cloth to remove any dirt or greasy marks. Paint with two coats of furniture paint and let dry.

TIP

Use a ready-mixed paint or create your own. The soft vintage shade used here was created by mixing together equal parts of bright green and pale gray furniture paint.

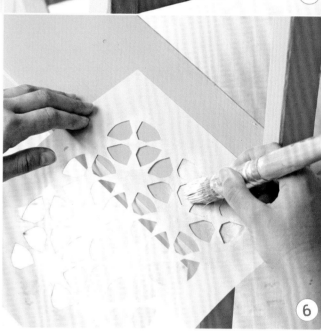

③

⑤

⑥

3 | When the paint has dried, apply a coat of varnish and let dry.

4 | Lightly coat the back of the stencil with spray adhesive. Position the stencil on one of the corners of the top step and smooth down. Alternatively, tape it in position. This stool is 14in (35cm) wide, and the repeat will fit perfectly if the outer edge of the design is aligned with the edge of the stool.

5 | Dip the tip of the stencil brush into the stencil paint and remove as much paint as possible on the side of the pot. Using a small circular motion, apply the paint through the holes. Lift the stencil and reposition, overlapping the design as shown. Repeat until the top of the stool is completely covered with the pattern.

6 | Position the stencil on the bottom step and repeat the process. You will need to bend the stencil back into the corners to get around the legs. Alternatively, you could just stencil a border across the width of the lower step, avoiding the need to tackle tricky corners.

7 | If you wish, apply a couple more coats of varnish over the steps for added durability.

NAIVE CHILD'S *chair*

When I buy old furniture I often wonder about its previous life. This little wooden chair had been painted and distressed, and had presumably been sent to the thrift store because its little owner had grown too big for it. I have no idea who will use this chair next, but there is something very satisfying about re-inventing a piece of discarded furniture and giving it a new lease of life.

MATERIALS AND EQUIPMENT

STENCIL (TEMPLATE ON PAGE 124)

CHILD'S WOODEN CHAIR

CLOTH

BRUSHES FOR PAINT AND VARNISH

WHITE FURNITURE PAINT

MATTE FINISH WATER-BASED VARNISH

TAPE MEASURE AND PENCIL

SPRAY ADHESIVE OR LOW TACK TAPE

BRIGHT GREEN ACRYLIC PAINT

PLASTIC POT OR OLD PLATE (FOR THE PAINT)

STENCIL BRUSH

STICKY NOTES

1 | Using the template on page 124, prepare the stencil following the instructions on page 10.

2 | Wipe down the chair with a damp cloth to remove any dirt or greasy marks, then apply two coats of white furniture paint. Start with the chair turned upside down to paint the legs and underside, then turn it over and paint the top side. Let dry.

3 | Apply a coat of varnish using a brush. Cover the whole chair and let dry.

4 | Using a tape measure, locate the center point of the chair seat and mark with a pencil.

5 | Lightly coat the back of the stencil with spray adhesive and lay on the chair with the pencil mark in the center of the motif. Alternatively, tape it in position. Pour a small amount of green acrylic paint into a plastic pot or onto an old plate. Dip the tip of the stencil brush into the paint, remove as much as possible on the pot or plate, then apply through the holes in the stencil.

6 | Reposition the stencil with the top tip of the motif just touching the bottom tip of the motif already painted. Apply the paint, then repeat at the top tip of the first motif. Place the stencil to one side of the central motif, again aligning the tips of the shapes. Apply the paint, then repeat on the other side.

7 | Reposition the stencil at each corner of the seat to complete the grid.

8 | Using sticky notes, mask all the shapes on the stencil apart from the small central flower. Place the stencil in a roughly centered position in the white spaces, then paint the little flowers in each space.

9 | Re-spray the back of the stencil with adhesive and position it in the center of the bar across the back of the seat. It may be helpful to lay the chair down to do this. If required, mask the two vertical shapes of the pattern with a sticky note. Apply the paint to the horizontal shapes and central flower, as shown.

metal
GARDEN TABLE

This folding metal garden table looks so much more interesting with the addition of a simple paisley border. The stencil paint I have used here works well on metal and is suitable for exterior use, but needs to be left for a day or so to harden off on such a smooth surface. If you make a mistake, it can be quickly wiped away with a damp cloth or baby wipe. The layout I have used works on the specific dimensions of this table, but the process can easily be adapted to fit any straight-sided surface.

MATERIALS AND EQUIPMENT

STENCIL (TEMPLATE ON PAGE 120)

METAL GARDEN TABLE—THE TOP OF THE ONE USED HERE MEASURES 27½ X 27½IN (70 X 70CM)

SPRAY ADHESIVE OR LOW TACK TAPE

TAPE MEASURE

STENCIL BRUSH

OFF-WHITE STENCIL PAINT

DAMP CLOTH OR BABY WIPES (OPTIONAL)

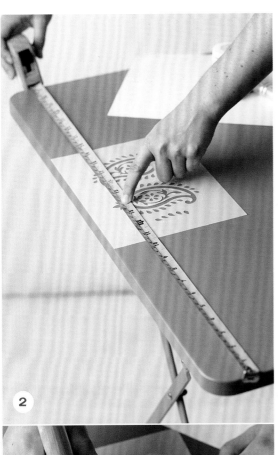

1 | Using the template on page 120, prepare the stencil following the instructions on page 10.

2 | Lightly coat the back of the stencil with spray adhesive. Place the upright paisley shape at the center point of one side of the table, using the tape measure as a guide. I positioned the bottom edge of my stencil along the edge of the table, but use the tape measure if you wish to position the border farther in or out from the edge of the table, or if your stencil is a different size. Alternatively, tape it in position.

3 | Dip the tip of the stencil brush into the paint, removing as much as possible on the side of the pot, then apply through the holes in the stencil in small circular movements.

4 | Carefully lift and reposition the stencil, overlapping the shapes, then apply the paint to create a centralized border of five paisley shapes. Repeat the same process along all four sides of the table.

5 | Position the stencil at a 45-degree angle in one of the corners and apply the paint. There is an element of positioning by eye here, but remember that if it looks unbalanced once the stencil has been lifted, you can simply wipe the paint away and repeat the process. Repeat this step for the remaining three corners.

monochrome
WASTE-PAPER BIN

The addition of this bold, folk-inspired motif has transformed this plain waste-paper bin into something with much more personality. I have used a black bent plywood bin for this simple project, but metal or plastic bins would also be suitable.

MATERIALS AND EQUIPMENT

STENCIL (TEMPLATE ON PAGE 118)
BLACK WASTE-PAPER BIN
SPRAY ADHESIVE AND LOW TACK TAPE
STENCIL BRUSH
CREAM STENCIL OR ACRYLIC PAINT

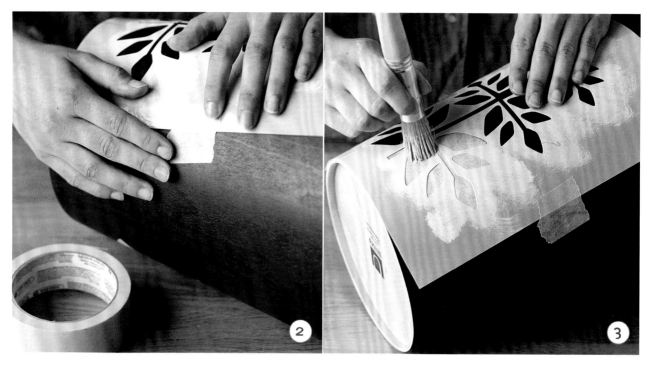

1 | Using the template on page 118, prepare the stencil following the instructions on page 10.

2 | Lightly coat the back of the stencil with spray adhesive, lay the bin on its side, then position the stencil. If the surface is curved, you will need to hold it in place with low tack tape. Check that the motif is straight by holding the bin upright.

3 | Dip the tip of the stencil brush into the stencil or acrylic paint and remove as much as possible on the side of the pot. Apply the paint through the holes in the stencil in a small circular motion. Carefully remove the stencil and let dry.

FURNITURE AND ACCESSORIES

industrial lamp
BASE

This lamp is a lovely blend of modern and retro industrial styles, with its filament light bulb, toggle switch, and contemporary white pattern on the bare wood. This is a quick and easy project, which can also be adapted for more conventional wooden lamp bases. For ease, I would recommend keeping to a flat-sided base rather than a cylindrical one.

MATERIALS AND EQUIPMENT

STENCIL (TEMPLATE ON PAGE 121)

WOODEN LAMP BASE

SPRAY ADHESIVE OR LOW TACK TAPE

RULER (OPTIONAL)

STENCIL BRUSH

WHITE STENCIL OR ACRYLIC PAINT

1 | Using the template on page 121, prepare the stencil following the instructions on page 10.

2 | Lay the lamp base on one side. Lightly coat the back of the stencil with spray adhesive and place it in the center of the base. Alternatively, tape it in position. You should be able to judge this by eye, but if you are unsure use a ruler to locate the center point.

3 | Dip the tip of the stencil brush into the stencil or acrylic paint, removing as much as possible on the side of the pot, then apply through the holes in the stencil with a small circular motion.

4 | Lift the stencil and reposition to the left side so that it overlaps the stenciled triangles. Apply the paint, then repeat on the right side.

5 | Continue the same process on each side of the lamp base, remembering to begin with the stencil in a centralized position each time.

MATERIALS AND EQUIPMENT

STENCIL (TEMPLATE ON PAGE 123)

WOODEN CRATES—THE ONES USED HERE MEASURE 16 X 12 X 7IN (40 X 30 X 18CM)

SPRAY ADHESIVE OR LOW TACK TAPE

TAPE MEASURE

STENCIL BRUSHES (ONE FOR EACH COLOR)

SOFT GREEN, BLUE, AND GRAY STENCIL PAINT

SMALL PAINTBRUSH

pretty storage CRATES

Keeping my studio organized and having easy access to my stuff is always a bit of a battle. I often find myself searching through brown cardboard boxes, trying to find an essential tool or piece of inspiration. Crates stack well and by stenciling each one a different color it is much easier to remember what is stored inside them. I always love a bit of color coding! The crates used here were bought new and have a lovely limed finish to the wood, but vintage crates are also great for this project and you can even use the lightweight fruit crates that grocery stores often throw away.

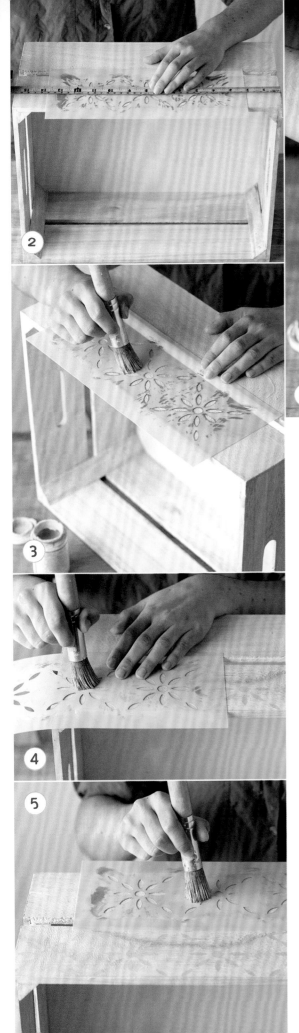

1 | Using the template on page 123, prepare the stencil following the instructions on page 10.

2 | Lightly coat the back of the stencil with spray adhesive and place roughly in the center of the first panel. Use the tape measure to locate the center point and adjust the position of the stencil if necessary. Alternatively, tape it in position.

3 | Dip the tip of one of the stencil brushes into the green stencil paint, remove as much as possible on the side of the pot, then apply the paint in a small circular motion through the holes in the stencil.

4 | Reposition the stencil with the outer shape overlapping the last flower painted. Apply the paint as before.

5 | Continue around the crate, adding the pattern to each panel on all sides, and always beginning at the center point of each side.

6 | To finish, paint the top edge and inside the handles with a small paintbrush. Decorate two more crates in the same way, using the blue and gray paints.

CHAPTER 2

FABRICS

chevron VINTAGE BAGS

A new leather handbag can be expensive and so is probably not something on which to experiment, but thrift-store finds are perfect for this project. The bags used here are made from a combination of suede and leather, but you can also use PU leather or canvas bags. By adding this simple pattern with a fast-drying stencil paint, the bags have been quickly transformed into something much more special. I have used this stencil to create horizontal and vertical patterns, but it would also look great used on the diagonal.

MATERIALS AND EQUIPMENT

STENCIL (TEMPLATE ON PAGE 116)

HANDBAG

CLOTH

SUEDE BRUSH (OPTIONAL)

SPRAY ADHESIVE OR LOW TACK TAPE

STENCIL BRUSH

WHITE STENCIL PAINT

1 | Using the template on page 116, prepare the stencil following the instructions on page 10.

2 | Wipe the leather with a damp cloth and, if your bag has suede parts, brush with a suede brush to remove dust and dirt. If you are using a canvas bag, there is no need to prepare the surface (unless it is dirty, in which case wash and iron the bag).

3 | Lightly coat the back of the stencil with spray adhesive. Smooth the stencil into position on the left side of the bag for vertical chevrons, or the top of the bag for horizontal chevrons. Alternatively, tape it in position. Dip the tip of the stencil brush into the stencil paint, removing any excess on the side of the pot. Using a circular motion, apply the paint through the holes in the stencil.

4 | Carefully lift the stencil and reposition, overlapping the last chevron painted, and continue across the bag until complete.

TIP

If the leather has a smooth surface, it will only need light pressure when applying the paint. Suede will require a little more pressure, as it has a textured surface.

dish TOWELS

Hand-decorated dish towels make lovely gifts. In fact, I have given most of my friends and family a stenciled dish towel at some point! Occasionally somebody will comment that they are too special to use, but once the ink has been fixed with a hot iron, they are machine washable, so really are meant for every day. I've used an Indian-inspired stencil to create different borders for this project, but, as it is a repeating design, it could also be used to create an all-over pattern.

MATERIALS AND EQUIPMENT

STENCIL (TEMPLATE ON PAGE 124)

COTTON OR LINEN DISH TOWELS—
THE ONES USED HERE ARE MADE
FROM LINEN AND MEASURE
18½ X 29IN (47 X 74CM)

IRON AND IRONING BOARD

SCRAP PAPER

SPRAY ADHESIVE OR LOW TACK TAPE

WHITE, TEAL, BLACK, AND ORANGE
FABRIC SCREEN-PRINTING INK

STENCIL BRUSHES (ONE FOR
EACH COLOR)

STICKY NOTES

1 | Using the template on page 124, prepare the stencil following the instructions on page 10.

2 | Iron the dish towel and lay it down flat. Protect your surface by placing some scrap paper beneath the towel in case the ink bleeds through the fabric.

3 | Lightly coat the back of the stencil with spray adhesive and position the stencil on the towel, with the bottom row of motifs running just above the hemline. The shapes at the side should overlap the edge. Smooth down the stencil so that it adheres to the fabric. Alternatively, tape it in position.

4 | Dip the tip of one of the stencil brushes into the white ink, remove any excess on the side of the pot, then apply in a small circular motion through the shapes of the top three rows of the design. Wash and dry the stencil. Using a different stencil brush, apply the teal ink to the bottom row in the same way.

5 | Wash and dry the stencil once more. Reposition on the dish towel one row up, so that it overlaps the white shapes, as shown. Apply the teal ink to the top row of shapes.

6 | Repeat the same process at the other end of the dish towel, and allow the ink to dry. Once dry, fix the color with a hot iron.

7 | To make a co-ordinating set of three dish towels, use the black and orange inks with the white ink. Vary the layout on each dish towel, as shown in the upper photograph on page 44.

SUZANI-STYLE
pillows

It has been mooted in my family that there might be too many pillows on our sofas, but I disagree! Pillows can completely change the look of a room, while incurring very little cost, especially if you stencil the covers yourself. Co-ordinate colors with an existing scheme or add some bold contrast. This stencil is inspired by the beautiful Suzani textiles originating from Central Asia. It is designed to be rotated around the central flower, to create the full circular pattern.

MATERIALS AND EQUIPMENT

STENCIL (TEMPLATE ON PAGE 123)

CANVAS PILLOW COVERS—THE ONES USED HERE ARE 17¾ X 17¾IN (45 X 45CM)

IRON AND IRONING BOARD

SPRAY ADHESIVE OR LOW TACK TAPE

SCRAP PAPER

STENCIL BRUSHES (ONE FOR EACH COLOR)

ORANGE, PINK, AND BLACK FABRIC SCREEN-PRINTING INK OR ACRYLIC PAINT

STICKY NOTES

③

④ ⑤ ⑥

1 | Using the template on page 123, prepare the stencil following the instructions on page 10.

2 | Fold the pillow cover in half and then in half again, and iron in the creases. Open out on a clean, flat surface and smooth out. The creases will indicate the center point and provide guidelines for positioning the stencil.

3 | Lightly coat the back of the stencil with spray adhesive and position on the cover, with the flower placed centrally over the center point. Lay a clean piece of scrap paper over the stencil, then smooth down again so that all the areas of the stencil adhere well to the fabric. Alternatively, tape the stencil in position.

4 | Dip the tip of one of the stencil brushes into the orange ink or paint, then apply in a circular motion through the first hole, as shown in the photograph above.

5 | Repeat the same process with the pink paint, then the black paint, using sticky notes to mask areas as necessary and following the photographs.

6 | Lift the stencil, rotate by 90 degrees, then position it by overlapping the shapes that have already been painted.

7 | Again, lay a piece of scrap paper over the stencil first, and smooth. Paint in the remaining areas, then repeat the process until the whole design is complete. If you have used fabric screen-printing ink, the color needs to be fixed by pressing the cover with a hot iron.

⑦

SCANDI-FOLK
napkins

I love to set a table with a theme, and these bold Scandi-inspired napkins create a real statement. The ones used here are new, but a selection of mismatched vintage napkins would also be gorgeous and the theme could be continued onto a tablecloth or runner. If you are using vintage napkins, make sure they have been washed and ironed before you start. Cotton or linen fabric will take the ink really well and, once ironed, can be machine-washed. This classic color combination of red and white works beautifully with simple white crockery and plain glasses.

MATERIALS AND EQUIPMENT

STENCIL (TEMPLATE ON PAGE 116)

NAPKINS—THE ONES USED HERE ARE
16 X 16IN (40 X 40CM)

IRON AND IRONING BOARD

SCRAP PAPER

SPRAY ADHESIVE OR LOW TACK TAPE

MARKER PEN

STENCIL BRUSH

RED FABRIC SCREEN-PRINTING INK

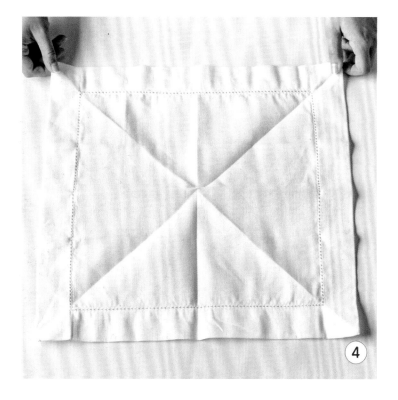

1 | Using the template on page 116, prepare the stencil following the instructions on page 10.

2 | Fold each napkin in half and then in half again, smoothing down the creases. Press the napkins first and fold them while still warm; that way the creases will be more visible.

3 | With the center point of the napkin facing toward you, take the two outer edges and fold them again to create a triangle, smoothing down again to create the crease.

4 | Open out the napkin and place it on a piece of clean scrap paper to protect the surface beneath.

5 | Lightly coat the back of the stencil with spray adhesive. Position the stencil in one of the quarters of the napkin and smooth down. Use the diagonal crease as a guideline to position the stem of the flower. Alternatively, tape it in position. With a marker pen, mark the corners of the stencil to indicate the edge of the napkin. You will now have a clear guide for repositioning the stencil.

6 | Dip the tip of the stencil brush into the ink and apply through the holes in the stencil in a circular motion. You will need a reasonable amount of ink on the brush, but make sure it is evenly distributed to avoid unsightly blobs.

7 | Lift the stencil and continue in the same way in each quarter of the napkin. Let dry, then press with a hot iron to fix the ink.

VINTAGE DENIM
jacket

Denim is a wonderful fabric for customization—an old jacket can be turned into something special with just a single motif stencil and some metallic silver paint. For this project, I have used a relaxed, random layout and deliberately stenciled over some of the seams to create an imperfect, broken motif.

MATERIALS AND EQUIPMENT

STENCIL (TEMPLATE ON PAGE 119)

DENIM JACKET

SPRAY ADHESIVE OR LOW TACK TAPE

TUBES OF METALLIC SILVER ACRYLIC PAINT

PLASTIC POT OR OLD PLATE (FOR THE PAINT)

STENCIL BRUSH

SCRAP PAPER

TIPS

When working on a random layout like this, I don't usually plan it out beforehand, preferring to build up the design gradually. I add one motif at a time and stand back to look at the balance before adding the next one. If you would rather plan the layout in advance, stencil the motif onto a piece of paper, photocopy it several times, then position the images on the jacket.

Acrylic paint is waterproof once dry and, unlike fabric paints and inks, you do not need to fix the color with a hot iron.

1 | Using the template on page 119, prepare the stencil following the instructions on page 10.

2 | Wash the jacket if necessary and let dry. Lightly coat the back of the stencil with spray adhesive, position at an angle on one of the sleeves of the jacket, and smooth down. Alternatively, tape it in position.

3 | Squeeze a little of the silver paint into a plastic pot or onto an old plate. Dip the tip of the stencil brush into the paint, rotating it on the surface of the pot or plate to remove any excess, then apply the paint through the holes of the stencil in a small circular motion.

4 | Lift and reposition the stencil, then repeat the process until you are happy with the design. If you stencil a motif over a seam, it is a good idea to blot the stencil between two pieces of paper afterward to remove any paint that may have bled underneath the stencil.

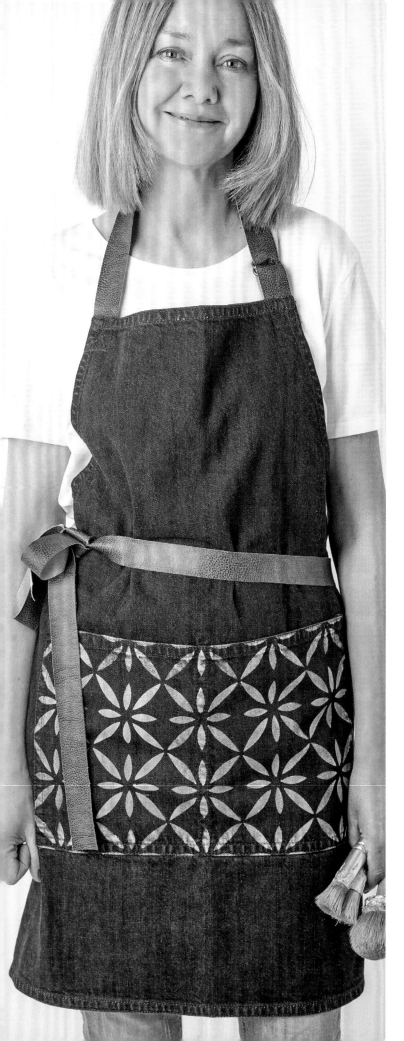

BATIK-INSPIRED
apron

When denim is stenciled with a white medium it creates an effect that is evocative of the indigo-dyed batik fabrics I love. This stencil was inspired by a huge batik bedspread that I brought home from India several years ago. It has been used on the pocket only for this project, but is designed to work equally well as a border or repeating pattern if your apron does not have a pocket. I used a white screen-printing ink which is specifically designed for fabric, but an acrylic paint is a good alternative.

MATERIALS AND EQUIPMENT

STENCIL (TEMPLATE ON PAGE 116)

APRON

IRON AND IRONING BOARD

SPRAY ADHESIVE OR LOW TACK TAPE

STENCIL BRUSH

WHITE FABRIC SCREEN-PRINTING INK

SCRAP PAPER

1 | Using the template on page 116, prepare the stencil following the instructions on page 10.

2 | If you are using an old apron, wash and iron it before beginning the project. The pocket on this apron had a center seam, which I used as a guide for positioning the stencil. If your apron does not have a seam, fold the apron in half from side seam to side seam and smooth down to create a crease, which can be used as a guide.

3 | Lightly coat the back of the stencil with spray adhesive. Lay your stencil down on the apron, using the seam or crease as a guide. Alternatively, tape it in position.

4 | Dip the tip of the stencil brush into the ink and remove any excess on the side of the container. Using a small circular motion, push the ink down through the holes of the stencil onto the fabric.

5 | Carefully lift the stencil and reposition. There is no need to wait for the ink to dry. In order to achieve a seamless repeat, place the stencil so that it overlaps the pattern that has already been painted.

6 | When adding the design to the edges of the pocket, put a piece of paper underneath the stencil to mask any fabric which you don't want to be stenciled. Finally, using a hot iron, press the stenciled design to fix the ink.

TIP

Woven fabric has a slightly uneven surface which requires a little more paint on the brush than when working on furniture. I therefore always recommend coating the back of the stencil with a spray adhesive. This ensures that the stencil adheres well to the surface and minimizes the risk of the paint bleeding underneath.

MEXICAN-INSPIRED
canvas bag

This project was inspired by the vibrant floral embroideries that can be found on vintage Mexican dresses. The use of different colors means that you will need to mask different areas of the stencil, and this takes time, but the results are worth the extra care. This is a project to approach when you want to treat yourself to a lovely therapeutic afternoon of stenciling!

MATERIALS AND EQUIPMENT

STENCIL (TEMPLATE ON PAGE 122)

CANVAS BAG—THE ONE USED HERE IS 29 X 14IN (47 X 35CM)

IRON AND IRONING BOARD

SPRAY ADHESIVE OR LOW TACK TAPE

STICKY NOTES

RED, BLACK, YELLOW, GREEN, AND TURQUOISE ACRYLIC PAINT

PLASTIC POTS OR OLD PLATE (FOR THE PAINT)

STENCIL BRUSHES (ONE FOR EACH COLOR)

1 | Using the template on page 122, prepare the stencil following the instructions on page 10.

2 | Wash the bag if necessary and let dry. Fold the bag in half and then in half again, and press the creases with a hot iron. Unfold the bag and lay it on a flat surface.

3 | Lightly coat the back of the stencil with spray adhesive and position the stencil in the top right quarter of the bag, with the central flowers overlapping the vertical central crease. The bottom flower should be just above the horizontal crease, as shown. You will need to flip the stencil and spray the other side at a later stage, so take a moment to work out which side to spray first by checking the photograph. Alternatively, tape it in position.

4 Using the sticky notes, mask the shapes around the central red flower. Pour a little red paint into a plastic pot or onto an old plate. Dip the tip of one of the stencil brushes into the red paint and rotate on the bottom of the pot or plate to remove any excess paint. With a small circular motion, fill in all the red areas, using the photograph as a guide. Repeat the same process for each color, using a new brush each time.

5 Lift the stencil and reposition it in the bottom left quarter of the bag (turning it 180 degrees, as shown in the photograph), before repeating the process described in Step 4.

6 Wash and dry the stencil, then flip it over and lightly coat the other side with the spray adhesive. Position in the top left quarter of the bag so that it overlaps the central red and turquoise flowers. Alternatively, tape it in position. Continue as before until the remaining two quarters have been filled in.

4

5

6

FLORAL
drapes

A pair of basic drapes (curtains) can be turned into something much more personal with the addition of some stenciled pattern. The positioning of the border across the bottom can be tailored to fit the dimensions of your windows. I have used a neutral color palette for this project, with a lovely pop of intense yellow ochre to frame the edges of the pattern, but you can, of course, use any palette that will fit your chosen room.

MATERIALS AND EQUIPMENT

STENCIL (TEMPLATE ON PAGE 122)

PAIR OF DRAPES (CURTAINS)—THE ONES USED HERE ARE A NATURAL-COLORED, COTTON-LINEN MIX

STICKY NOTES

SPRAY ADHESIVE OR LOW TACK TAPE

SCRAP PAPER

STENCIL BRUSHES (ONE FOR EACH COLOR)

WHITE AND YELLOW OCHRE FABRIC SCREEN-PRINTING INK

IRON AND IRONING BOARD

1 | Using the template on page 122, prepare the stencil following the instructions on page 10.

2 | Decide where you would like your horizontal border to start, and mark the position with a sticky note.

3 | Lightly coat the back of the stencil with spray adhesive and place it at the top of the drape (curtain) with the outer column of flowers overlapping the edge, as shown above. Alternatively, tape it in position. Place a piece of paper underneath to protect the work surface.

4 | Dip the tip of one of the stencil brushes into the yellow ochre ink and apply to the single overlapping column of flowers. Continue down the outer edge until you reach the sticky note. Wash and dry the stencil (see page 11).

5 | Reposition the stencil at the top of the drape, overlapping the yellow ochre flowers, then apply the white ink with a clean, dry stencil brush. Continue down the side to the required length, remembering to leave the bottom row of flowers unpainted, as these will be added in the next step using the yellow ochre ink. Repeat the process from the top of the drape. The width of the border can be adapted to fit your drapes, but I have made mine four white flowers wide.

6 | Create the horizontal border by repeating the same process with the white ink across the width of the fabric. I have painted three rows of white flowers here, but again, the border can be made deeper by adding additional rows.

7 | Wash and dry the stencil again before adding the bottom row of flowers with the yellow ochre ink. If you wish, the vertical border can also be added to the other side of the drape.

8 | Repeat the same layout on the other drape remembering to begin on the opposite side, so that the design will be symmetrical where the drapes meet in the middle. Finally, press the fabric with a hot iron.

TIPS

You could also use fabric or stencil paint.

You will need a reasonably large work surface for this project, but if you don't have a suitable tabletop, work on the floor instead. It needs to be a hard surface, rather than a carpeted floor.

WOODBLOCK EFFECT
bedlinen

Stenciling a whole duvet cover is a real labor of love, but a deep border is easily achievable and the finished results make it well worth the effort. This woodblock-inspired stencil has been used in a simple grid repeat. For a looser pattern, simply place it at different angles on the fabric. I recommend using fabric screen-printing ink for this project. Once ironed and washed, it will produce a lovely soft handle, which will fare well in the washing machine.

MATERIALS AND EQUIPMENT

STENCIL (TEMPLATE ON PAGE 123)

COTTON BEDLINEN SET—THE ONE USED HERE IS
FOR A TWIN BED

IRON AND IRONING BOARD

SPRAY ADHESIVE OR LOW TACK TAPE

STENCIL BRUSHES (ONE FOR EACH COLOR)

BLUE AND WHITE FABRIC SCREEN-PRINTING INK

SMALL CONTAINER WITH A LID AND SPOON
(FOR MIXING COLORS)

SCRAP PAPER

1 | Using the template on page 123, prepare the stencil following the instructions on page 10.

2 | Locate the center point at the top of the duvet cover by folding it in half. If you wish, you can press the crease in with an iron. Lightly coat the back of the stencil with spray adhesive, then place squarely over the crease line at the top of the cover, centering the stencil over the crease. Alternatively, tape it in position.

3 | Dip the tip of the stencil brush into the blue fabric ink and remove as much ink as possible on the side of the pot. Apply the ink through the holes in the stencil in a small circular motion.

4 | Continue across the width of the cover, butting the tips of the motif together. Repeat on the next row, again butting the tips of the motif together to create a grid layout. I stenciled three rows of dark blue shapes here, but this can be adjusted depending on how deep you wish the border to be. Wash and dry the stencil.

5 | Place four spoonfuls of white ink into a small container, then add half a spoonful of blue ink and stir thoroughly to make a paler blue shade.

6 | Position the stencil in one of the spaces at the top of the duvet cover, ensuring that the tips of the motifs are just touching. Use a piece of paper to protect your work surface where the stencil hangs over the edge. Apply the light blue ink with a dry stencil brush, as before.

7 | Stencil the remaining spaces with the light blue ink.

8 | Repeat the whole process on the pillowcases. Once the ink is dry, press all the stenciled areas with a hot iron to fix the ink.

TIPS

You can also use fabric paints, although these tend to come in small pots, so might not be practical for a large project.

When mixing inks, note down the quantity of each color used, so that the same shade can be mixed again. The size of the spoon doesn't matter—what's important is to remember the ratio of colors used. When I was at college, we used to record our color recipes and put a sticker on the side of the jar.

LAYERED *wall art*

This is a project where you can really improvise and have some fun. Feel free to combine different kinds of paint which you may already have available. I have used furniture paint with a matte finish, combined with the soft sheen of a turquoise acrylic paint and the high shine of a metallic bronze paint. You could also use leftover emulsion or eggshell paints. Try grouping together three canvases with varying layouts and a different color balance. The stencil is an Indian-inspired Sarasa motif that's often found on block-printed textiles. It is designed to be placed at different angles, with small elements that can be used to fill in empty areas of the canvas.

MATERIALS AND EQUIPMENT

STENCIL (TEMPLATE ON PAGE 121)

PLAIN WHITE BOX CANVAS—THE ONE USED HERE IS 14 X 11IN (35 X 27.5CM)

SELECTION OF PAINTS (SEE TIP ON PAGE 65)

PAINTBRUSH

SCRAP PAPER

SPRAY ADHESIVE OR LOW TACK TAPE

STENCIL BRUSHES (ONE FOR EACH COLOR)

PLASTIC POTS OR OLD PLATE (FOR THE PAINT)

1 | Using the template on page 121, prepare the stencil following the instructions on page 10.

2 | Paint the whole canvas, including the sides, with the light blue paint and let dry.

3 | Use two pieces of clean paper to mask out a rectangle on the bottom left of the canvas. Holding the paper in position and using the dark blue paint, place the paintbrush on the edge of the paper and brush downward onto the canvas. This will create a clean edge. Remember to also paint down the sides, again using the paper as a mask. Paint a dark blue rectangle on the top right of the canvas using the same technique.

4 | Using clean paper, mask the remaining rectangles on the top left and bottom right of the canvas, then paint with the bright turquoise acrylic and let dry.

5 | Lightly coat the back of the stencil with spray adhesive and place on the bottom right side of the canvas so that it is overlapping the dark blue rectangle. Alternatively, tape it in position. Dip the tip of the stencil brush into the white stencil paint, remove as much as possible on the side of the pot, and then apply the paint through the holes in the stencil using a small circular motion. Repeat until all areas of white pattern are completed. Wash and dry the stencil.

6 | Add the top layer of stencil pattern, using the metallic bronze acrylic paint and a dry stencil brush.

upholstered
DINING CHAIR

Old, upholstered wooden dining chairs can easily be found in junk stores, and are such good candidates for a bit of creative reinvention. This chair looked very dated, with the seat covered in a worn purple fabric and a dark brown, shiny varnished frame. You can make a feature of a single chair in a hallway or bedroom, or group together mismatched chairs which have been given the same treatment around a dining table. I have created a regular layout of pattern here, but the width between the columns of leaves can be increased or decreased, and the design can also be applied in an irregular layout.

MATERIALS AND EQUIPMENT

STENCIL (TEMPLATE ON PAGE 117)

WOODEN DINING CHAIR WITH
REMOVABLE UPHOLSTERED SEAT

FURNITURE PAINT

MATTE VARNISH

BRUSHES FOR THE PAINT
AND VARNISH

FABRIC—I USED 20 X 20IN
(50 X 50CM), SEE TIP ON PAGE 68

FABRIC SCISSORS

IRON AND IRONING BOARD

SCRAP PAPER

SPRAY ADHESIVE OR LOW TACK TAPE

STENCIL BRUSH

SOFT GREEN STENCIL PAINT

HEAVY-DUTY STAPLE GUN

1 │ Using the template on page 117, prepare the stencil following the instructions on page 10.

2 │ Remove the seat from the frame of the chair and clean the wood with warm, soapy water. Remove the fabric from the seat and set it aside, as this will be used as a template for the new cover.

3 │ Apply two coats of paint to the frame of the chair and let dry. Check the drying time between coats on the instructions on the side of the can. It is much easier to paint the legs and the underside with the frame turned upside down and placed on a work surface or tabletop.

4 │ Once the paint is dry, apply a couple of coats of varnish and let dry.

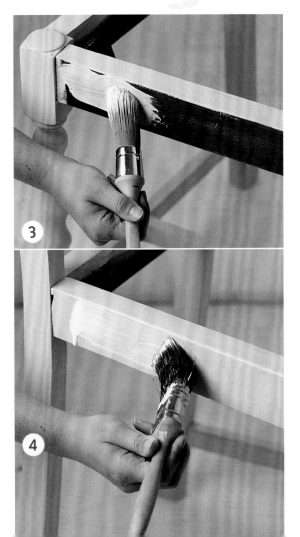

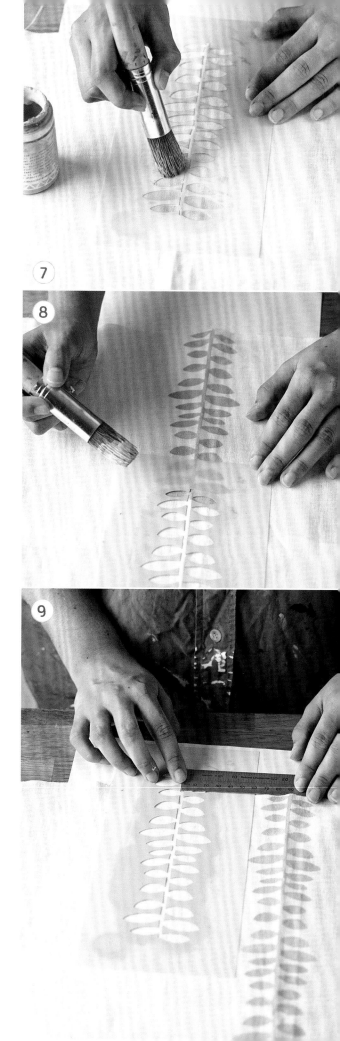

5 Lay out the new fabric on the work surface and place the old fabric on top. Use this as a template to cut around. There is no need to be too precise, as the fabric can be trimmed once it has been stapled to the base. You can now discard the old fabric.

6 Press the fabric using a hot iron, then fold in half from side to side and lightly iron in a central crease. Place a piece of scrap paper underneath the fabric to protect your work surface.

7 Lightly coat the back of the stencil with spray adhesive and place on the fabric with the stem of the leaf design positioned over the central crease line. Align the bottom of the stencil with the bottom edge of the fabric. Alternatively, tape it in position. Dip the tip of the stencil brush into the paint and, after removing any excess, apply the paint in a small circular motion.

8 Lift the stencil and reposition so that the bottom two leaves overlap the top two stenciled leaves. Repeat the same process at the top of the panel.

9 Measuring along the bottom of the fabric, move the stencil across so you have a gap of 3½in (9cm) between the stems, then move it down from the edge of the fabric by a couple of leaves. This will create a more interesting and irregular pattern as the leaves will not be repeated in parallel.

TIP

There are a few things to consider when choosing fabric for this project. Ideally, it should be a medium-weight fabric without stretch. If the fabric is too thick, it may be difficult to drop the seat back into the frame. If it is too thin, it will wear and possibly tear. The fabric used here, although a good weight, was a little transparent, so I covered the dark wadding on the seat with a piece of old sheet before stapling the stenciled fabric on top.

10 | Apply the paint as before, then repeat the process across the width of the fabric.

11 | Lay the fabric face down on the work surface, placing the seat on top in a roughly centered position. Fold the fabric up and over the sides, using the leaf design on either side as a guide for finding the central positioning.

12 | Staple along one side of the frame, then pull the fabric taut on the opposite side and staple it into position.

13 | Repeat on the remaining two sides, pinching the fabric at the corners, but leaving it unstapled until the end.

14 | Open out and flatten the pinched fabric at the corners, then staple flat. Trim off any excess material, then drop the seat into the chair frame. Don't worry if the fit is a little tight, you can always sit on it to ease it into position!

TIP

You can also use fabric paint or fabric screen-printing ink, but you will need to fix the medium with a hot iron.

CHAPTER 3

GIFTS
AND HOMEWARE

MOROCCAN-INSPIRED
lampshade

The repeat-pattern stencil used for this project has a Moroccan-inspired motif often seen in screens and mosaic tiles. The color palette can easily be adapted to co-ordinate with an existing color scheme within your home. Lampshade-making kits are readily available, but generally you will need to supply your own fabric. I used an old white cotton sheet. Although sheeting fabric is relatively lightweight, once it is attached to the backing supplied in the kit, it works beautifully. You can play around with the layout and positioning of this stencil to create an all-over pattern or a central border.

MATERIALS AND EQUIPMENT

STENCIL (TEMPLATE ON PAGE 117)

LAMPSHADE-MAKING KIT—THE ONE USED HERE HAS A 12-IN (30-CM) DIAMETER AND AN 8½-IN (21-CM) HEIGHT

FABRIC—I USED COTTON, BUT MOST FABRICS WITH A SMOOTH SURFACE ARE SUITABLE

TAPE MEASURE

SCISSORS

IRON AND IRONING BOARD

SCRAP PAPER

SPRAY ADHESIVE OR LOW TACK TAPE

2 STENCIL BRUSHES (OPTIONAL: ONE LARGE AND ONE SMALL)

BLUE FABRIC SCREEN-PRINTING INK

METALLIC GOLD ACRYLIC PAINT

STICKY NOTES (OPTIONAL)

1 | Using the template on page 117, prepare the stencil following the instructions on page 10.

2 | Cut the fabric to the dimensions stated in the kit instructions. If using vintage fabric, make sure it is clean before beginning the project. Press with a hot iron, then fold the top and bottom edges together, smoothing along the length of fabric to create a central guide line for positioning the stencil. Place on a piece of paper to protect the surface you are working on.

3 | Lightly coat the back of the stencil with spray adhesive and position so that it overlaps the edge of the fabric with the crease running through the middle row of holes. Alternatively, tape it in position. Dip the tip of one of the stencil brushes into the blue ink, then apply through the holes in the stencil in a small circular motion. Regularly reload the brush with ink in order to achieve a lovely saturated color. Leave the top and bottom rows of motifs unpainted.

4 | Using a smaller stencil brush, if you have one, fill in the remaining rows with the metallic gold paint. You may find it helpful to mask the blue pattern with sticky notes or scrap paper to protect them from the gold paint.

5 | Carefully lift the stencil and reposition, overlapping the shapes already painted. Continue along the length of the fabric and let dry before pressing with a hot iron.

6 | Follow the kit instructions to apply the fabric to the backing and roll it around the frame.

SOUTHWESTERN
notebooks

Notebooks make lovely gifts, particularly when a little time has been taken to personalize them. My friends and family have received so many stenciled notebooks from me over the years, often tied with string into little bundles. A single motif stencil is very versatile and can be used to create lots of different patterns by playing around with the layout. The Southwestern-inspired stencil used for this project was positioned differently on each book, creating a lovely co-ordinating trio. I used a color palette of white combined with pink and turquoise, chosen to match the notebook covers, but this stencil also works well as a one-color design.

MATERIALS AND EQUIPMENT

STENCIL (TEMPLATE ON PAGE 118)

SELECTION OF NOTEBOOKS—THE ONES USED HERE ARE 7 X 10¼IN (18 X 26CM)

SCRAP PAPER

STICKY NOTES (OPTIONAL)

SPRAY ADHESIVE OR LOW TACK TAPE

SMALL STENCIL BRUSHES (ONE FOR EACH COLOR)

WHITE, TURQUOISE, AND PINK STENCIL PAINT

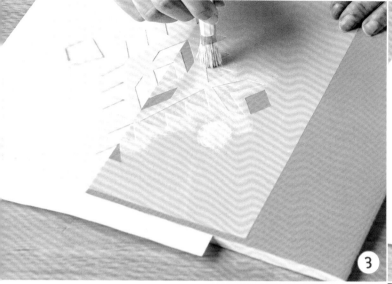

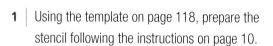

1 | Using the template on page 118, prepare the stencil following the instructions on page 10.

2 | Place a piece of paper underneath the front cover of the first notebook to protect the edges of the pages below. Lightly coat the back of the stencil with spray adhesive and position it with half of the design overlapping the edge on the right-hand side of the book. Alternatively, tape it in position. There is no need to use a ruler, just place the stencil by eye using the shapes in the design as guides.

3 | Dip the tip of one of the stencil brushes into the white paint and remove as much as possible on the side of the pot. Apply the paint with a small circular motion, picking out specific areas of the pattern, either using the photograph as a guide for color placement or choosing your own.

4 | Using another brush dipped in the turquoise paint, repeat the same process through the remaining holes. There is no need to wait for the white paint to dry first.

5 | Carefully lift the stencil and place it in the same position on the left-hand side of the book. Smooth down, or tape in position. Apply the paint, repeating the same layout as before.

6 | Reposition the paper to protect the pages at the top of the book. Place the stencil so that it overlaps the top half of the cover and repeat the same process used on the sides. Finally complete the bottom section.

7 | Vary the position and colors of the stenciling on the other notebooks to create a set (see page 75). The paint dries quickly and there will be very little build-up, so it shouldn't be necessary to wash the stencil between notebooks.

TIPS

If you are using tape to secure the stencil, it is especially important
that it is a low tack tape, to avoid marking the cover.

A smaller stencil brush will make it easier to isolate specific shapes,
but you may also find it helpful to protect painted areas with scraps of
paper or sticky notes.

tribal cards
AND GIFTWRAP

The stencil used in this project is based on a collection of tribal-inspired lino-cuts I created a few years ago. I have used a three-color layout here, but it is a very versatile design, which can be used in many different ways. You could try a combination of more than three colors, or just keep it simple with one color.

MATERIALS AND EQUIPMENT

STENCIL (TEMPLATE ON PAGE 125)

PACK OF BLANK KRAFT PAPER
GREETINGS CARDS

ROLL OF BROWN KRAFT PAPER
(OR SEVERAL LARGE SHEETS)

SPRAY ADHESIVE OR LOW TACK TAPE

STICKY NOTES

SMALL STENCIL BRUSHES
(ONE FOR EACH COLOR)

PINK, BLACK, AND WHITE STENCIL
OR ACRYLIC PAINT

SCRAP PAPER

(2)

(3)

TO STENCIL THE CARDS

1 | Using the template on page 125, prepare the stencil following the instructions on page 10.

2 | Lightly coat the back of the stencil with spray adhesive and place on one side of the card, as shown. This will be the front of the card. Alternatively, tape it into position.

3 | Using the sticky notes, mask the areas surrounding the shapes that are to be painted pink. Dip the tip of the stencil brush into the pink paint and, after removing any excess paint, apply in a small circular motion through the shapes, as shown.

4 | Mask the areas around the shapes to be painted black with sticky notes, then repeat the process with a new, dry stencil brush. Cover the shapes that you are not using with a piece of paper. This will protext the back of the card.

5 | Finally, repeat the process to paint the remaining shapes in white.

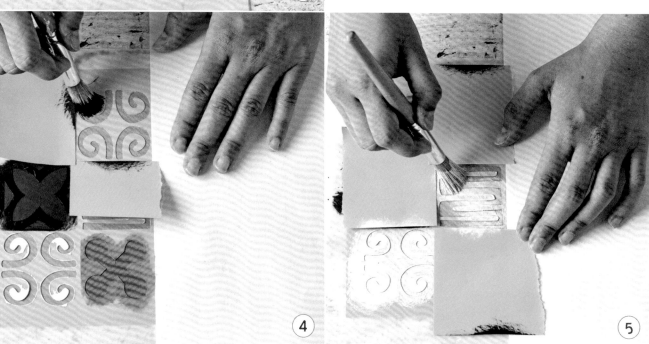

(4)

(5)

TO STENCIL THE GIFTWRAP

1 | Lightly coat the back of the stencil with spray adhesive as before, and position the stencil so that the shapes are aligned with the edge of the paper. Alternatively, tape it into position. Repeat the process used for the cards, masking the shapes and painting each color in turn. The paint dries quickly, and there will be very little build-up, so it shouldn't be necessary to wash the stencil before using it again.

2 | Lift the stencil and move it up, repositioning it farther along the edge of the paper. Overlap the triangle at the top of the stencil with the white triangle which has been painted and align the shapes at the side with the edge of the paper. Continue working along the edge of the paper until you've filled the whole width.

3 | Returning to the top of the paper, position the stencil so that the triangle overlaps the black triangle which has already been painted. Repeat the previous steps until the whole area of the paper has been covered with pattern.

TIP

If you are using a roll of paper, it may be useful to tape the edges onto your work surface using low tack tape. This will prevent the paper from rolling back up as you are working.

glass STORM LANTERN

A stenciled storm lantern with a large church candle burning in it would make a lovely table centerpiece. You can use any glass vase or lantern, or even a large jar for this project, as long as the area to be stenciled has straight sides. This is such a quick and simple project, but it transforms basic glass containers into something much more interesting. They look great grouped together in varying sizes with a different layout on each. The stencil paint used here is suitable for interior and exterior use and will withstand being wiped over with a damp cloth or rinsed under a faucet (tap)—but not being scrubbed.

MATERIALS AND EQUIPMENT

STENCIL (TEMPLATE ON PAGE 125)

STRAIGHT-SIDED GLASS LANTERN OR VASE, OR LARGE JAR

SPRAY ADHESIVE AND LOW TACK TAPE

STENCIL BRUSH

WHITE STENCIL PAINT

1 | Using the template on page 125, prepare the stencil following the instructions on page 10.

2 | Lightly coat the back of the stencil with spray adhesive and bend it around the container. It will also need to be held in position with a piece of low tack tape on either side.

3 | Dip the tip of the stencil brush into the paint and remove as much paint as possible on the side of the pot. Using a small circular motion, apply the paint through the holes in the stencil.

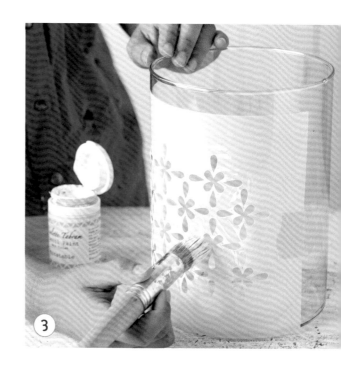

4 | Unpeel the tape, lift the stencil, and reposition it, overlapping the painted shapes in the outer column. Tape the stencil in place again and apply paint as before.

5 | Repeat until you have worked all the way around your container. Leave a small space between the edges of the pattern, as it is unlikely that the container will be the precise diameter needed to create a seamless repeat.

NEON GEOMETRIC
skateboard

This old-school skateboard was the perfect candidate for some customization using a simple geometric pattern stencil and some neon paint. I was really pleased with the finished item, though far too nervous to actually stand on it! The pink areas were selected to create random pops of bright contrasting color, but you could also plan a more formal layout in advance on a piece of paper.

MATERIALS AND EQUIPMENT

STENCIL (TEMPLATE ON PAGE 121)

SKATEBOARD

CLOTH

SPRAY ADHESIVE OR LOW TACK TAPE

STENCIL BRUSHES (ONE FOR
EACH COLOR)

NEON YELLOW AND NEON PINK
ACRYLIC PAINT

STICKY NOTES

1. Using the template on page 121, prepare the stencil following the instructions on page 10.

2. If you are using an old skate-board, wipe with a damp cloth to remove any dirt or greasy marks.

3. Lightly coat the back of the stencil with spray adhesive and place over one end of the skateboard, smoothing it into position. Alternatively, tape it in position.

4. Dip the tip of one of the stencil brushes into the neon yellow paint, removing as much as possible on the side of the pot and making sure the paint is evenly distributed along the bristles. Apply the paint through the holes in the stencil in a small circular motion.

5. Lift the stencil and reposition so that the edge overlaps the pattern which has already been painted. This will create a seamless repeat. Continue until the area is complete, then repeat at the other end of the skateboard. Wash and dry the stencil.

6 | Reposition the stencil in the central area between the wheels. Tear small pieces of the sticky notes to mask the areas which are to be painted pink, making sure that you use the part of the note with the sticky end. Paint the unmasked areas of the stencil with neon yellow.

7 | Discard the pieces of sticky note, while keeping the stencil in position. Using fresh sticky notes, mask the yellow areas surrounding the unpainted holes. Dip the tip of the clean stencil brush into the neon pink paint, removing as much as possible as before, and fill in the remaining holes in the stencil.

8 | Carefully lift and reposition the stencil, repeating the same process until the panel is complete.

RELIEF STENCILED
mirror

The lovely raised pattern on these mirror frames has been created using stencil paste which has been applied through the stencil. Once dry, it can be painted and, as here, given a distressed finish. When I use the paste on furniture, I don't usually sand the edges, but I think the effect looks beautiful on these mirrors. The stencil used here is a repeating pattern and, therefore, this project requires a little patience, as the paste needs time to dry before the stencil can be overlapped. The finished results are well worth it, though.

MATERIALS AND EQUIPMENT

STENCIL (TEMPLATE ON PAGE 120)

SMALL MIRROR WITH WIDE FLAT FRAME—THE ONES USED HERE MEASURE 10¼ X 10¼IN (26 X 26CM)

SPRAY ADHESIVE OR LOW TACK TAPE

RELIEF STENCIL PASTE

FLAT WOODEN STICK OR PALETTE KNIFE

SCRAP PAPER

BLUE AND GREEN PAINT— I USED FURNITURE PAINT

MATTE FINISH WATER-BASED VARNISH

BRUSHES FOR THE PAINT AND VARNISH

SANDPAPER (SEE TIPS BELOW)

TIPS

It is preferable to use a Mylar® stencil with stencil paste as it is a much more durable material.

You can use an old credit card to apply relief stencil paste.

Fine-grade sandpaper creates a subtly distressed effect which can be built up gradually.

1 | Using the template on page 120, prepare the stencil following the instructions on page 10.

2 | Lightly coat the back of the stencil with spray adhesive and position it at the bottom of one side of the frame. Alternatively, tape it in place. Scoop out some of the relief paste using a flat wooden stick or palette knife, then, holding the stencil in place with one hand, start to apply the paste.

3 | Smooth the paste over the stencil in a thick layer. Imagine that you are icing a cake. There is no need for the paste to be perfectly smooth on top.

4 | Hold the stencil at both ends, then carefully lift it upward. Place it on a piece of scrap paper, scrape off the excess paste, and return this to the pot.

5 | Repeat on the opposite panel, then set aside and wash and dry the stencil. The drying time for the paste will vary depending on the room temperature and how thickly it has been applied, but it should take roughly an hour. Check the manufacturer's instructions. Once the paste is dry, reposition the stencil by overlapping some of the shapes which have hardened, then complete the remaining length on each of the two side panels. Let dry.

6 | Repeat the same process in the middle section of each of the remaining panels and let dry.

7 | Apply paint over the whole frame, pushing it down into the little nooks created by the paste. Let dry.

8 | Apply a coat of varnish and, again, let dry.

9 | Gently pass the sandpaper over the surface of the frame in a circular motion, and along the edges, checking regularly until the desired level of distressing has been achieved. Using a dry paintbrush, sweep any remaining dust into a trash can.

Christmas cards
AND GIFTWRAP

Each December I spend a lazy Sunday afternoon in my studio stenciling Christmas cards and giftwrap. It is a tradition which I absolutely love: listening to the radio with a scented candle burning and eating the odd mince pie. I become so completely absorbed that my children know to warn me of their approach, with a little cough or heavy footsteps. The snowflake stencils for this project are very versatile and could be used in lots of different ways. I have used a simple Scandinavian palette of red and white, but metallics on dark paper could be very cool, or try neon brights on white for a clean, modern vibe.

MATERIALS AND EQUIPMENT

STENCILS 1, 2, AND 3
(TEMPLATES ON PAGE 125)

PACK OF PLAIN WHITE CARDS—
THE ONES USED HERE ARE 6 X 6IN
(15 X 15CM)

ROLL OR PIECES OF PLAIN
WHITE GIFTWRAP

SPRAY ADHESIVE OR LOW TACK TAPE

SCRAP PAPER

STENCIL BRUSH

RED STENCIL OR ACRYLIC PAINT

RULER (OPTIONAL)

Using the template on page 125, prepare the stencils following the instructions on page 10.

CARD 1: REGULAR LAYOUT

1 | Lightly coat the back of Stencil 1 with spray adhesive. Place the unfolded card on a piece of paper and position the stencil in the center of the front. Alternatively, tape it in position.

2 | Dip the tip of the stencil brush into the paint, removing as much as possible on the side of the pot, then apply in a small circular motion through the stencil holes.

3 | Carefully lift the stencil, then repeat, to create a row of three snowflakes, with the tips of each motif just touching. The snowflake on the left side will overlap the crease line on the card—this will look lovely once it has been folded in half.

4 | Reposition the stencil at the bottom of the card so that the edge overlaps and the top tip of the motif is just touching the snowflake above. Continue along the row, then repeat at the top of the card.

CARD 2: TOSSED LAYOUT

1 | Lightly coat the back of Stencil 2 with spray adhesive. Place the unfolded card on a piece of paper. Position the stencil off-center and at a slight angle on the front of the card. Alternatively, tape it in position. Apply the paint in a small circular motion.

2 | Either use the same stencil again, or choose a different one. Position the second stencil at a slightly different angle at the side of the first snowflake, so that it is overlapping the edge of the card, then apply the paint through the stencil.

3 | Continue working around the first motif, alternating the snowflake shapes and adjusting the angles as you go. There is not a right or wrong way to do this—have fun and enjoy the process!

GIFTWRAP 1:
REGULAR LAYOUT

1 Lightly coat the back of Stencil 1 with spray adhesive. Place the giftwrap flat on the work surface. Begin by placing the stencil squarely in one of the corners of the paper. Alternatively, tape it in position. Apply the paint in a small circular motion.

2 Continue adding the snowflakes, running down the edge of the paper. If you wish, you can measure the spacing between each motif with a ruler, although I tend to do this by eye. Once the paper is wrapped around a gift, it won't be noticeable if your spacing is uneven (and even if it is, it really doesn't matter). Repeat across the width of the paper.

GIFTWRAP 2:
TOSSED LAYOUT

1 Lightly coat the back of Stencils 2 and 3 with spray adhesive. Place the giftwrap flat on the work surface. Begin in one of the corners, placing the stencil at an angle before applying the paint. Alternatively, tape it in position.

2 Reposition the stencil, rotating the angle a little. Continue across the surface of the paper, changing the angle of the stencil each time, and allowing roughly the same spacing.

TIP

I have only used one of the snowflake motifs for each sheet of paper in the photographs above, but a combination of all three would work beautifully as well.

MATERIALS AND EQUIPMENT

STENCIL (TEMPLATE ON PAGE 120)

BLACK PICTURE FRAME—THE ONE USED HERE IS 15 X 15IN (38 X 38CM)

SPRAY ADHESIVE OR LOW TACK TAPE

TAPE MEASURE

STENCIL BRUSHES (ONE FOR EACH COLOR)

CREAM AND SOFT GREEN STENCIL OR ACRYLIC PAINT

MOROCCAN TRELLIS
picture frame

This picture frame has a wide, flat surface, which is perfect for embellishing with a stenciled pattern. Although it is made from plastic, it looks so much more expensive with the addition of this Moroccan-inspired pattern.

1 | Using the template on page 120, prepare the stencil following the instructions on page 10.

2 | Lightly coat the back of the stencil with spray adhesive, then place on the bottom panel of the frame so that it is roughly centered. Use the tape measure to locate the center and adjust the positioning if necessary. Alternatively, tape it in place.

3 | Dip the tip of one of the stencil brushes into the cream stencil or acrylic paint, remove as much as possible on the side of the pot, then apply through the holes in the stencil.

4 | Reposition the stencil at one end of the border, overlapping the shapes which have already been painted. Fill in the pattern, then repeat on the opposite side. Using the same process, stencil the pattern across the width of the top panel.

5 | Place the stencil on one of the side panels in a centered position and apply the cream paint as before. Lift and repeat on the other side panel.

6 | Lay the stencil over the edge of one of the sides so that the tops of the shapes fill the gaps, as shown in the photograph. Apply the soft green paint with a dry stencil brush and continue on all outer and inner edges.

little CERAMIC POTS

A collection of little pots is a lovely way to display small succulents or windowsill herbs. The ones I have used here were bought as a set, but mismatched containers in different sizes and materials can also look great. This is a quick and simple project using a small, irregular triangle border.

MATERIALS AND EQUIPMENT

STENCIL (TEMPLATE ON PAGE 118)

GROUP OF POTS

SPRAY ADHESIVE AND
LOW TACK TAPE

STENCIL BRUSHES (ONE FOR EACH COLOR)

CREAM AND GRAY STENCIL PAINT

SCRAP PAPER

1 | Using the template on page 118, prepare the stencil following the instructions on page 10.

2 | Lightly coat the back of the stencil with spray adhesive and place it on the top of the pot. If you are using a round pot, it will also be necessary to fix the stencil in position on either side with some low tack tape.

3 | Dip the tip of one of the stencil brushes into the paint and remove as much as possible on the side of the pot. Rotate the brush on a piece of paper to remove any excess paint.

4 | Apply the paint in a small circular motion, then carefully lift the stencil and reposition, overlapping the last triangle at the side. Continue around the circumference of the pot. It is unlikely that the pattern will meet in a perfect repeat, so either leave a small gap or overlap the design a little if necessary.

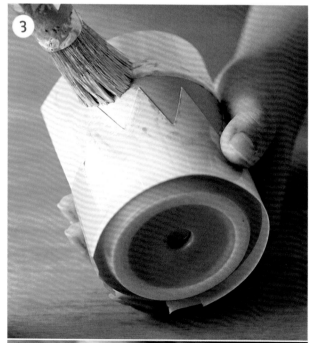

mosaic

BAMBOO COASTERS

While coasters have a very practical purpose, to me they also offer the perfect surface for adding some pattern. I've used a stencil that is inspired by the small mosaic tiles found in so many of the rich, decorative cultures to which I am drawn. The layout of the color has been alternated here, but a different bold color on each coaster would also look gorgeous.

MATERIALS AND EQUIPMENT

STENCIL (TEMPLATE ON PAGE 121)

A SET OF COASTERS—THE ONES USED HERE ARE
MADE FROM BAMBOO AND MEASURE 4 X 4IN
(10 X 10CM)

SPRAY ADHESIVE OR LOW TACK TAPE

RULER AND PENCIL (OPTIONAL)

STICKY NOTES

STENCIL BRUSHES (ONE FOR EACH COLOR)

WHITE AND CORAL STENCIL OR ACRYLIC PAINT

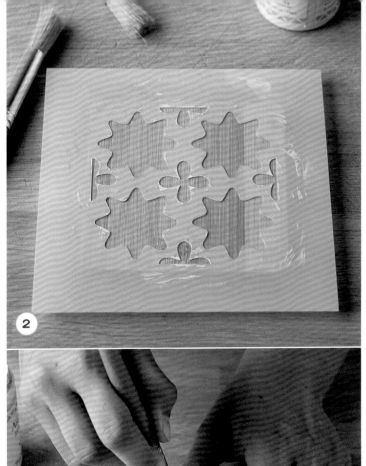

1 | Using the template on page 121, prepare the stencil following the instructions on page 10.

2 | Lightly coat the back of the stencil with spray adhesive and place it squarely on the coaster. Alternatively, apply low tack tape on the underside. You can use a ruler and pencil to measure and mark the center point if you wish, though I usually do this by eye.

3 | Mask the areas around the larger shapes with sticky notes. Dip the tip of one of the stencil brushes into the white paint and remove as much paint as possible on the side of the pot. Apply the paint to the four large shapes with a circular motion.

4 | Mask the white areas with sticky notes, then fill in the remaining shapes with the coral paint using a new stencil brush.

TIP

You could also use coasters made from different materials—try slate or cork.

CHAPTER 4

WALLS
AND FLOORS

CONTEMPORARY *tiles*

I love mismatched patterned tiles and this project shows how one simple design can be used in different ways on natural stone and ceramic tiles. The stencil paint I have used is perfect for tiles which are not going to be exposed to water or need heavy cleaning. For bathrooms and kitchens I would advise using a specific tile paint. The template for this stencil can be enlarged or reduced in scale so that it will fit a specific tile size.

MATERIALS AND EQUIPMENT

STENCIL (TEMPLATE ON PAGE 119)

TILES

CLOTH (OPTIONAL)

SPRAY ADHESIVE OR LOW TACK TAPE

STENCIL BRUSH

STENCIL PAINT—THE ONE USED HERE IS SUITABLE FOR BOTH INTERIOR AND EXTERIOR USE

STICKY NOTES

TIP

The hard, non-porous surface of the tiles requires very little paint. It is advisable to remove as much paint as possible from the brush, onto a piece of paper, before applying it to the tile.

1 | Using the template on page 119, prepare the stencil following the instructions on page 10.

2 | If you are stenciling onto tiles that are already in situ, make sure they are free from dirt and greasy marks by wiping with a damp cloth before beginning.

3 | Lightly coat the back of the stencil with spray adhesive. Position the stencil diagonally on the tile, then smooth down. Alternatively, tape it in position.

4 | Dip the tip of the stencil brush into the paint and remove as much as possible on the side of the pot. Apply the paint through the holes in the stencil in a small circular motion.

5 | Carefully lift the stencil and reposition it so that you have one ellipse in a corner. Mask the edge of the shape above with a sticky note, then apply the paint. Repeat for each of the corners.

6 | Another option is to position the stencil squarely on the tile, as shown in the photographs. This creates a different effect. You could even use sections of the design on a rectangular tile.

metallic
WALLPAPER TRIO

The use of metallic colors on these wallpapers creates a rich, glamorous vibe, making them perfect for a feature wall. Working directly on the roll of paper, I have used this versatile motif stencil to create a different layout for each paper. Stencil a little more than the required drop, before cutting each length of paper with a scalpel and metal ruler. Then repeat the same layout on the next length.

MATERIALS AND EQUIPMENT

STENCIL (TEMPLATE ON PAGE 124)

ROLL OF GOOD-QUALITY LINING
WALLPAPER—THE ONE USED
HERE IS 2000 GRADE AND 20½IN
(52CM) WIDE

LOW TACK TAPE

SCRAP PAPER

TAPE MEASURE

MARKER PEN OR PENCIL

SPRAY ADHESIVE

TUBES OF METALLIC BRONZE, SILVER,
AND GOLD ACRYLIC PAINT

PLASTIC POTS OR OLD PLATE
(FOR THE PAINTS)

STENCIL BRUSHES (ONE FOR
EACH COLOR)

SCALPEL AND METAL RULER (FOR
CUTTING THE LENGTHS
OF WALLPAPER)

GETTING STARTED

1 | Using the template on page 124, prepare the stencil following the instructions on page 10.

2 | This project is best worked on a long table (ideally a wallpaper table), but you can work on the floor if you don't have one available. Use the low tack tape to hold the paper in position on the table or floor. This will prevent it from rolling up.

3 | You will need to mark the center of your paper for the bronze and silver layouts, using scrap paper (this is so that you don't have to mark the lining paper). See page 106.

BRONZE PAPER LAYOUT

1 | Place a piece of scrap paper roughly in the center of your lining paper, just underneath one end. Fix in position with low tack tape. Use the tape measure to locate the center point of the lining paper and mark it with a dot on the scrap paper.

2 | Lightly coat the back of the stencil with spray adhesive. Using the dot on your scrap paper as a guide, position the stencil so that the motif is centered, with half of the design overlapping the edge of the lining paper. Smooth it down so that it adheres to the paper. Alternatively, tape it in position.

3 | Squeeze a little bronze paint into a plastic pot or onto an old plate, then load a brush, rotating it on the bottom of the pot or plate in order to distribute the paint along the bristles. Using a small circular motion, apply the paint through the stencil holes.

4 | Carefully lift the stencil and reposition, so the tip of the bottom shape just touches the top tip of the bronze motif. Apply the paint through the stencil as before, and continue along the length of the paper, occasionally using the tape measure to check the center point.

TIPS

You can also stencil directly onto paper that has already been hung, beginning at the top and working downward.

For a more intense metallic finish, I would recommend using tubes of acrylic paint, rather than pots, which tend to be less opaque.

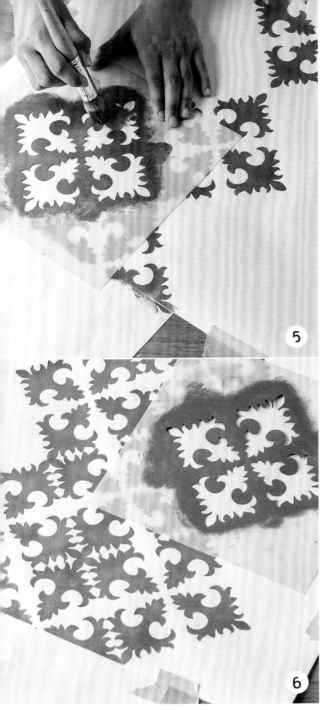

5 | Position the stencil on the left side of the stenciled motif with the bottom tip touching the edge of the paper and the tip on the right side just touching the bronze motifs in the central column, as shown. Apply the paint as before, then continue in the same way along the length of the paper.

6 | Complete the layout on the other side of the central motif in the same way.

2

3

4

5

SILVER PAPER LAYOUT

1 Mark the center of your paper (see Step 1, page 106). Lightly coat the back of the stencil with spray adhesive. Use the dot on the scrap paper as a guide to center the stencil, this time with the whole motif on the paper. Smooth the stencil down. Alternatively, tape it in position.

2 Squeeze a little silver paint into a plastic pot or onto an old plate, then load a brush, rotating it on the bottom of the pot or plate in order to distribute the paint along the bristles. Using a small circular motion, apply the paint through the stencil.

3 Place a second piece of scrap paper beneath the lining paper on one side and tape in position. Place the stencil over the side of the paper, with half of the motif overlapping the side edge, as shown above.

4 Apply the silver paint to the half of the stencil that is sitting on the lining paper. Mark the top edge of the stencil with a dot on the scrap paper, as shown. My stencil measures 10 x 10in (25 x 25cm) but if yours is a different size, the dot should be 2¼in (6cm) from the edge of the motif.

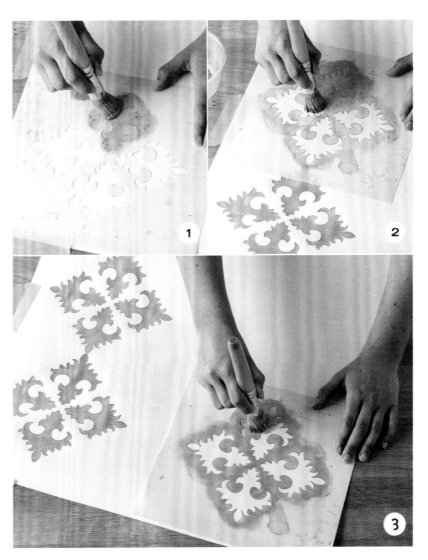

5 | Reposition the stencil so that the bottom edge is aligned with the dot on the scrap paper (there should be a gap of 2¼in/6cm between the bottom tip of the motif and the top tip of the motif already stenciled). Apply the silver paint as before. Continue along the side of the paper.

6 | Repeat the same process on the opposite side of the paper, then complete the central column using the motifs on either side as a guide for the placement of the stencil, aiming for the center. Finally, fill in the remaining design by placing the stencil squarely within each space.

GOLD PAPER LAYOUT

1 | Lightly coat the back of the stencil with spray adhesive. Position the stencil in one corner of the paper and smooth down. Alternatively, tape it in position. The outer edge of the motif should be positioned 1in (3cm) in from the edge of the paper. Dip the brush into the gold paint and it on the bottom of the pot or plate to remove excess paint. Apply the paint in a small circular motion through the stencil holes.

2 | Lift the stencil and reposition, with the tip of the bottom shape just touching the top tip of the gold motif. Align the side of the stencil with the edge of the paper. Apply the paint and continue along the length of paper.

3 | Position the stencil in the opposite corner of the paper and work down the other side of the paper, as before.

MONOCHROME
Dhurrie rug

Originating from India, a dhurrie rug is made from cotton using a flat-weave technique. This creates a relatively smooth surface suitable for stenciling. I have used a simple bold motif for this project with a monochrome color palette. The layout of the pattern covers the whole of the rug, but you could also stencil a simple border across each end. Fabric screen-printing inks are great for stenciling rugs as they are the perfect consistency, suitable for covering larger areas, and they can also be mixed together easily to create new colors.

MATERIALS AND EQUIPMENT

STENCIL (TEMPLATE ON PAGE 117)

COTTON RUG WITH A FLAT WEAVE—
THE ONE USED HERE IS 24 X 47IN
(60 X 120CM), BUT YOU CAN USE ANY
SIZE AND ADJUST THE LAYOUT OF THE
PATTERN ACCORDINGLY

TAPE MEASURE (OPTIONAL)

WHITE AND BLACK FABRIC SCREEN-
PRINTING INK

SMALL PLASTIC POTS AND SPOON

SPRAY ADHESIVE OR LOW TACK TAPE

STENCIL BRUSH

LARGE PIECE OF SCRAP PAPER

IRON (OPTIONAL)

1 | Using the template on page 117, prepare the stencil following the instructions on page 10.

2 | Use a tape measure or fold the rug in half, then quarters, to create crease lines which can be used as a guide to work out the positioning of the stencil on the rug. Place the stencil centrally along the vertical creases. You could also measure the rug and sketch out the positioning and spacing for the stencil in advance, if you prefer.

3 Mix the black and white inks to create the two tones of gray. It is important to measure the ratio of colors so that you can recreate the color should you run out. I used three parts black and one part white for the darker gray and one part black and three parts white for the lighter gray. Use a spoon to measure the ink each time and mix in a small plastic pot. Give the ink a good stir to mix the colors.

4 Lightly coat the back of the stencil with spray adhesive and, starting at one end, smooth into position so that it adheres well to the rug. Alternatively, tape it in position.

5 Load the stencil brush with the dark gray fabric ink and, using a circular motion, push the ink down into the weave of the fabric through the holes in the stencil. In order to minimize the possibility of the ink bleeding underneath the stencil, position the loaded brush in the center of the shapes and work out toward the edges of the motif.

6 Continue along the length of the rug, then use the same process to fill in the gaps along the center.

7 Wash and dry the stencil, then place a large piece of paper beneath the rug to protect the surface below. Position the stencil so that only half of the design is on the rug. Use the outer tips of the shape as a guide to align the stencil. With a clean, dry stencil brush, apply the lighter gray ink along the outer edges. Once dry, press with a hot iron to fix the ink if you wish to be able to machine-wash the rug.

TIP

When mixing colors, measure and take a note of the proportions used so that the same color can be created again if you run out before the end of a project.

TILE-INSPIRED
floor

The floors upstairs in my house are covered in a pattern that I have stenciled onto painted floorboards. It is a cheap way to add interest and disguise less-than-perfect boards (like mine!). The surface used in this project is a painted plywood, but the technique can also be used on lino, concrete, or even on unpainted floorboards. You can also reverse the color layout I have used here by painting two shades of gray onto a white background. I usually begin floor projects by placing the stencil against the edge along a wall, then continuing across the room. Floorboards can be used as guides to keep the design true. Remember to take the time to stand back occasionally and review your work.

1 | Using the template on page 123, prepare the stencil following the instructions on page 10.

2 | Prepare the surface by vacuuming and washing the whole area. If you are painting the surface before stenciling, then apply two coats of floor paint with a brush or roller. Allow to dry, following the guidelines on the pot for drying times between coats.

3 | Using the tape or sticky notes, cover the four teardrop shapes on the stencil, then lightly coat the back of the stencil with spray adhesive and position on the floor. Alternatively, tape it in position.

4 | Dip the tip of one of the stencil brushes in the white stencil paint, removing most of it on the side of the pot. Apply the paint through the unmasked shapes.

5 | Reposition the stencil with the outer tips of the shapes butted against each other. Continue in the same way across the whole surface.

6 | Remove the masks from the teardrop shapes, then wash and dry the stencil. Using more tape or sticky notes, mask just the areas of the stencil on either side of the points of the tear drops, as shown. Reposition the stencil over the white pattern and, using the gray paint, fill in the remaining shapes. Repeat across the whole floor area.

TIP

Most good-quality floor paints are hard-wearing, so do not require varnish. The acrylic stencil paint I used here does not require varnish either. If the paint does need the protection of varnish, apply one coat before the pattern is added, then a second coat afterward.

templates

All templates are printed at 50% and will need to be enlarged by 200% using a photocopier (or scanner and printer) before use.
For instructions on how to cut out and use stencils, see page 10.

Batik-inspired apron
page 52

Scandi-folk napkins
page 48

Chevron vintage bags
page 42

Concrete planter
page 20

Upholstered
dining chair
page 67

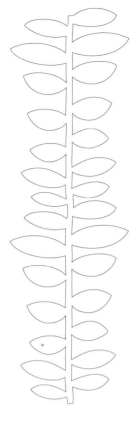

Monochrome Dhurrie rug
page 110

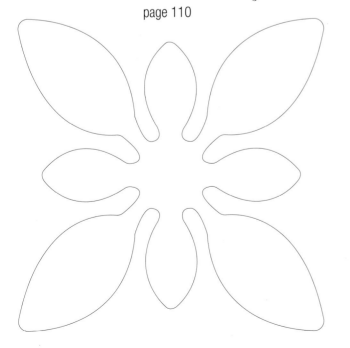

Moroccan-inspired lampshade
page 72

Southwestern notebooks
page 75

Monochrome waste-paper bin   page 34

Graphic floral chair
page 14

Little ceramic pots
page 96

Contemporary tiles
page 102

Vintage denim jacket
page 50

STENCIL 1

Decorative nightstand
page 17

STENCIL 2 (ALSO USED FOR THE INLAY EFFECT CABINET ON PAGE 23)

Inlay effect cabinet
page 23

Moroccan trellis picture frame
page 94

Relief stenciled mirror
page 87

STENCIL 1　　　　STENCIL 2

SEE ALSO STENCIL 2, PAGE 119

Metal garden table
page 32

Neon geometric skateboard
page 84

Layered wall art
page 63

Industrial
lamp base
page 36

Mosaic bamboo coasters
page 98

Step stool
page 27

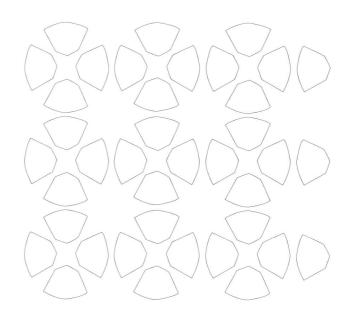

Floral drapes (curtains)
page 57

Mexican-inspired canvas bag
page 54

Pretty storage crates
page 38

Woodblock effect bedlinen
page 61

Suzani-style pillows
page 46

Tile-inspired floor
page 113

Dish towels
page 44

Naive child's chair
page 29

Metallic wallpaper trio
page 104

Tribal cards and giftwrap

page 78

Glass storm lantern

page 82

Christmas cards and giftwrap

page 91

STENCIL 1

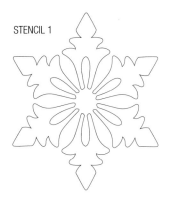

STENCIL 2

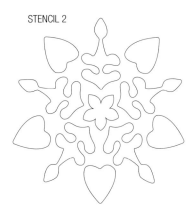

STENCIL 3

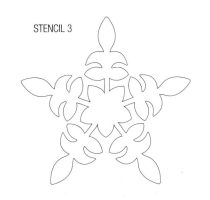

RESOURCES

Visit nicolettetabram.com for a wide range of stencils, brushes, stencil paste, and stencil paint. For stenciling tutorials, search for "Nicolette Tabram Designs" on youtube.com.

ikea.com is a great source for items that provide a blank surface for stenciling onto. The step stool (page 27), napkins (page 48), drapes (curtains) (page 57), bedlinen (page 61), notebooks (page 75), and mirror frames (page 87) all came from Ikea.

homesense.com (US, Canada, UK) is a great place for inspiration and quirky finds. You never know what you might find from one visit to the next. The apron (page 52) and picture frames (page 94) came from here and they usually have a good selection of stationery and notebooks.

thecleverbaggers.co.uk (UK-based but with international shipping) is a good online source for basic textiles. The dish towels (page 44), pillow covers (page 46), and canvas bag (page 54) are from there.

hobbycraft.co.uk (UK) is a good source for plain cards and box canvases. The wooden crates (page 38) also came from there.

ebay.com, craigslist.org (US/Canada), gumtree.com (UK), freecycle.com (UK), and preloved.co.uk (UK) are all good sources for second-hand furniture. Most of my purchases come from local thrift stores and I have learned that a good piece needs to be bought immediately. I have missed a few good pieces by waiting and returning to the store the following day.

homedepot.com (US/Canada), homebase.co.uk (UK), and B&Q (diy.com) (UK) are great for essential tools and materials such as low tack tape and lining paper.

cassart.co.uk (UK), joann.com (US), hobbylobby.com (US), and michaels.com (US/Canada) are great online sources for acrylic paints, fabric screen-printing inks, cutting mats, and craft knives.

amazon.com sells sheets of Mylar® suitable for cutting stencils.

INDEX

ACKNOWLEDGMENTS

I would like to say a huge thank you to Cindy Richards for seeing the potential in stencils and asking me to write this book. Thank you to everybody at CICO Books who has been involved in this project—Sally Powell; Anna Galkina, my calm and gentle editor; Kerry Lewis for her patience, guidance, and that blue shirt; and Amy Christian for her clarity.

Thank you to Terry Benson for his beautiful photography and great lunches and Jess Contomichalos for styling the shots. Thank you to Elizabeth Healey for her beautiful design.

I would also like to thank Mick Flinn from The Stencil Store, my friend and mentor for all of his advice. A massive thank you to my mum, dad, brother, and sister who just seem to believe in me.

And finally, a big thank you to my partner Jimmy and our children Conor and Mia for their support and encouragement. This book is for you. xxx